— PARENTS —
SEND YOUR CHILD
to College for Free®

3RD EDITION

— PARENTS —
SEND YOUR CHILD
to College for Free®
Successful Strategies that Earn Scholarships

3RD EDITION

TAMEKA L. WILLIAMSON

PARENTS, SEND YOUR CHILD TO COLLEGE FOR FREE, 3RD EDITION

Copyright © 2021 Tameka L. Williamson
All rights reserved.

Published by Publish Your Gift®
An imprint of Purposely Created Publishing Group, LLC

Printed in the United States of America

ISBN: 978-1-64484-522-6 (print)
ISBN: 978-1-64484-523-3 (ebook)

Special discounts are available on bulk quantity purchases by book clubs, associations, and special interest groups. For details email: sales@publishyourgift.com or call (888) 949-6228.
For information log on to www.PublishYourGift.com

Join the *College for Free* Movement

FB, IG, Twitter: @IamCoachTwill

YouTube Channel: /CoachTwill

Join My Email List & Receive Free Resources

tamekawilliamson.com

thecollegeprepboss.com

A Valuable Resource

"I found this book to be a valuable resource for high school students and their parents as they explore and prepare for post-secondary options."

—SHIRLEY C. KILGORE, ED.D., RETIRED PRINCIPAL/
EDUCATIONAL CONSULTANT

It's the Perfect "Go To" Resource for Families

"At a time when colleges are capping their enrollments to reduce costs, this guide provides a wonderful comprehensive overview of what it takes for students to strategically prepare for the college admissions process. It's the perfect "go to" resource for families wondering where to start."

—JESSICA JOHNSON, EXECUTIVE DIRECTOR, SCHOLARSHIP ACADEMY

An Excellent Guide for Children and Parents

"Tameka Williamson's college prep book is well-written. As a former University Coordinator who has worked with at-risk children at the University of Missouri, I think this book would be an excellent guide for children whose parents did not attend college and are not familiar with college life. I think Tameka has done a wonderful job; she has given the potential student an overview and a roadmap to college life, both academically and socially."

—MRS. D. KNIGHT, STAY-AT-HOME MOM

A Step-by-Step College Preparatory Guide

"The moment I saw the title for this book, I realized that I had never seen one like it. As teachers, parents, educators, and all who care for and work with children from all grade levels, we should begin to use terminology that acquaints children with upper level information, helping to create upward bound mindsets. We tend to think our children should wait until high school to learn what college preparation is all about. This is a step that should be taken by every grade level. Acquaint our young people about the vocabulary and terminology as soon as they begin to talk. This book does just that. An introduction to college at an early level gives children a mindset that something else is to come after "this." Tameka Williamson has outlined, extraordinarily well, steps for our young ones and their parents to take in preparing for college life. I will purchase many of these just to hand out to students and parents. This book will make wonderful gifts to students and parents in lieu of toys and clothes. They will be able to step it up, knowing that their steps are already ordered.

—Mrs. Johnson, Kansas City, Missouri

A Must-Read

"It is evident with this book that the author is an advocate of education. Ms. Williamson has a sincere passion to prepare parents, guardians, and youth as they seek higher educational opportunities. This book is quite unique because it focuses on middle school students as well as high school students. The author has done her due diligence in researching topics that are instrumental in preparing a young learner for advanced education. After reading this book, the reader will have a clear, concise and sound approach in developing a strategy for higher academia endeavors. This book is a must read."

—Donna Warfield Fareed, 2005 Amazon
bestselling author of *Whatever Floats Their Boat*

A Wonderful Tool for High School Students and Parents

"Congratulations to Tameka Williamson for the time, effort, and expertise devoted to this book. I feel that this book will help students grasp the realities of college life. This college preparatory and planning guide is a wonderful tool for college bound high school students and parents. I believe that it will benefit a lot of people whether they decide to pursue college or not."

—A. McLean, parent

A Book Full of Such Relevant Information

"The book was purchased for my granddaughter, but I also gained a lot from it. It should have been out when I started to go to college, and is full of such relevant information. It is well-written and gets straight to the point."

—Dr. Hunt, parent

TABLE OF CONTENTS

ACKNOWLEDGMENTS

I would first like to thank God for orchestrating my life with divine purpose.. He has positioned me to live with a mission that makes a difference in the lives of families and young people across the globe.

Thank you to my College for Free families for trusting me to guide and counsel you on how to make your college dreams a reality without all that debt. Helping to develop students and get them to a place of staying focused so they can seize every opportunity afforded to them is a role I am humbled by and don't take lightly. It is for this reason: everything I do and create is dedicated to God, my mentees, my families, and my tribe.

As always, I am grateful for the continued support of my sweetie and my parents. You've always had my back, all of you. A special shout out to my tribe and team for supporting the vision, challenging me at every level to be great, to stay focused, and to never give up or give into the negativity.

Tameka

FOREWORD

My Why...

God gives us this amazing gift in the form of life and we are held accountable for what we do with it. Linda Ellis' poem, *The Dash*, challenges people to reflect on how they will spend their life from the time they are born until the time they die. My goal is to be a good steward of the life entrusted to me and pour out everything I have while on this earth so that I can leave a legacy that keeps giving, allowing me to have poured out every last drop of myself when I perish. Therefore, I thank you for investing in your college bound family by reading my book. It is my hope that you are mentally challenged and intellectually stimulated so that your mindset shifts you from one of *getting* ready to one of *being* and *staying* ready. This requires a mindset shift and ownership of your family's future from beginning to end.

Get ready to learn that the key to killing the college game is owning everything associated with college admissions, financial aid, and scholarships. Although I don't fully dive into the strategies, as that is reserved for my VIP Coaching Clients, the foundational pieces regarding the process are laid out in the book. This is the first part of knowing the *who, what, when,* and *where* so that you can understand the *why*. Without this as your knowledge base, you will be struggling through the college admissions waters like a ship without a navigation system. It will lead you to a place called "anywhere," with a lifetime of debt that's not worth it.

I was a first generation college student with wonderful parents. They each had what was classified as a good job, yet with only high school diplomas. No, they are not college educated but the work ethic, values, principles, and discipline they instilled in me made me the formidable and compassionate business leader, professor, and entrepreneur I am today. These are the principles exemplified in the book. Although my parents were supportive of me and all my endeavors, including college, they didn't have the knowledge or understanding of the steps to take, the timing of those steps, guidelines, and rules that would get me through college without debt. Of course, they didn't have the funds to just write a check. So, we winged it and did the best we could with what was available at the time. Keep in mind that this was well over 25 years ago. The college game has drastically changed since then, and it's still changing, which is exactly why this book is necessary.

Between the library, a college resource center we had in Kansas City for students interested in going to college, friends going through the process with me, teachers, and organizations, I was able to at least map out a high level plan (application, career selection, and scholarships). Because of my diligence, I was awarded about $2,500 in scholarships prior to starting college, with $1,500 renewable each year. That number increased when I started doing research as a Timbuktu Scholar to add about $2,000 a year. Unfortunately, however, this was not enough. Granted, my Cost of Attendance (COA) gap was not astronomical, compared to the cost of attending college in today's world. My balance was covered by student loans (which I'm still paying for, but not for long; that is a life lesson for another day), with a little left over.

The other sad reality is that I could have been granted more money if I had started the process earlier, before my senior year, and had higher test scores. You see, I went to the top college-prep school in the state, where I had an unweighted 3.7 GPA. When you paired that with my test scores (ACT 19 and 20; my SAT score I can't remember because I fell asleep during the test), I didn't make the cut for an academic scholarship or acceptance into the Honor's College. This could have also prevented the awarding of other merit-based funds. My point is this: my lack of knowledge cost me opportunities that could have prevented the need for student loans. But my struggle at that time is now your guiding light.

Before moving forward, I want to debunk a myth I continue to hear in my practice and often see manifested on social media pages. The assumption that being an honor roll student should translate into money for college or even a free ride is one I need you to eliminate from your thinking. The average tuition and fees for the 2020-21 academic year increased by 1.1% to $10,560 for in-state students at four-year public colleges, according to College Board. The data also shows tuition and fees for private institutions increased by 2.1% to $37,650. Consequently, the expectation is that students will borrow more than $38,000 to cover the cost of their bachelor's degree (NerdWallet), propelling collective student loan debt in the US beyond $1.7 TRILLION. Ensuring that college is paid for requires a plan, discipline, a commitment to the process, and families starting early and fully owning the process. Remember, hope is not a strategy. Hoping your child's strong academic prowess will yield a full-ride opportunity will leave you and your child disappointed and in debt.

In case you don't believe me, let's take the example of the "Hopeful" Family (I've changed their name to protect their privacy). They reached out to me for help because their 4.32 GPA daughter with a 1320 SAT score was denied admissions to what she considered her dream school. Not only was she denied admissions to that school, but she was also denied admissions to three of the four schools she applied to. The one school she did gain acceptance to did not offer her a full-ride. Unfortunately, there wasn't much we could do because of many factors, one being timing. I was able to explain to her why it happened and offered some suggestions on how to reset. Because they followed my advice, more doors opened but not at the level they would have if the right approach was taken in the beginning. Unfortunately, this is not an isolated incident. So please take heed and apply the tips shared throughout the book.

My goal is to impart all I know to help families like yours send your child to college without the burden of student loan debt. With the debt crisis in this country and the requirement of some form of college education (trade/technical, two-year or four-year) in order for this generation to gain employment and make a livable wage, something must be done. Parents, I am here to serve as your College Positioning System, or CPS (instead of GPS), and help you learn how to avoid the college landmines, kill the college game and ultimately send your child to college for FREE!

Our proven methods and strategies have connected families across the world to over $75 million in scholarships and our private VIP Clients to well over $40 million in scholarships. I want the same for you. It won't happen overnight, and it requires some sweat equity.

ARE YOU READY?

HOW BAD DO YOU WANT IT?

THEN (as we say in Louisiana), LET'S GEAUX GET IT!

The College for Free™ journey will now begin with the College Prep Boss®.

The College Success Cycle

Prepare…

Plan…

Execute…

Monitor & Control…

Adjust…

Execute Again.

MESSAGE TO PARENTS

I decided to write this book because I wanted to provide you with a resource to equip you with the tools and knowledge needed for setting your college bound scholar up for success. It is NOT the high school counselor's job to get your child college and career ready. But they are part of the process and you need to partner with them along the way.

Whether it's a trade program, a professional certification (Google Professional, Apple, etc.), a technical college, the military, or a four-year institution, 90% of 21st century jobs will require some form of post-secondary education and training. Education, now more than ever, has become the tool that opens the door to countless opportunities. The key is to do it in a way that makes sense of dollars and cents.

Unfortunately, the current condition of our educational system has crippled our children, primarily minorities (Blacks and Hispanics), to be left behind physically, mentally, and intellectually. We as parents, communities, family units, and churches must take more of a united front and stand together by educating our children on how to garner post-secondary success without a life of bondage by being in debt. The process and full ownership of the process starts at home. No longer can we be complacent and live life on the sidelines, expecting the government and school districts to educate and prepare our kids. There must be steps taken sooner and intentionally in the home that elevates their learning experience, lessons to teach them how to be accountable for their learning and success, and educational professionals must be held accountable for effective subject-matter teaching. The goal here is not perfection but rather excellence, follow-through, and completion, inspiring them to be the best at every level, and not like everyone else. Our kids are our future and it's our responsibility as parents, mentors, and leaders to foster that safe learning and development environment for them.

You accomplish this by taking the time to invest in educating them not only on the basics, but by exposing them to global subjects (international exchange programs, learning multiple foreign languages, and learning about the global economy, for example), creating community initiatives, engaging in government and legislature issues, and financial literacy and comprehension. Also paramount are creating jobs and opportunities through entrepreneurship, and showing these kids how math and science can be fun to learn and will open doors for them in the years to come. In order for their futures to be bright, changes will need to be made in how we prepare them to compete in the current world we live in.

While working in Corporate America, I had the opportunity to recruit, interview, and mentor young adults. In doing this, coupled with my role as an Adjunct Professor, I constantly saw a lack of crucial skills like critical thinking, problem-solving, effective communication, and professional etiquette. An absence of any of these skills impacted their performance, upward mobility, and future opportunities. It's difficult to play catch up when you are constantly behind. The time to reset and reboot is overdue. The development of these kids must be intentional, built around vision, and facilitated through dedicated action.

Failure to course correct will yield a generation of passive, incompetent, and lost adults incapable of leading and passing the baton to the generation that follows them. One key to success as a generational leader is to pass the baton and set the next generation up to be and to do greater. As I examine the state of our country, there's a void in leadership and a greater need for our youth to be equipped to step up and redirect the efforts and energy put out in the world.

With the shift in the economy, there has been a clear line separating those unemployed with a degree and those jobless without a degree. The more the global economy focuses on a green environment, sustainable energy, science, technology, engineering, agriculture, art, and mathematics (STE(A)M), artificial intelligence (AI), and data analytics, the more critical it has become to create a workforce pipeline for these career fields. Parents, don't set your child up to miss the boat on this major shift that has taken place. Without proper preparation and a solid knowledge-base of the hot areas driving our country forward, our children will be part of the skills gap and ultimately left behind. As a result, they won't be able to compete and have secure, sustainable employment.

As your personal College Coach, this book is an extension of me, designed to provide you as parents, group counselors, youth, and mentors with a roadmap that outlines what is required to *Properly Plan to Prevent Poor Performance* (my essential 5 Ps) by your college bound scholar. Understanding the content in this book will bring clarity to the chaos that exists in the college admissions world. Our goal is not only to get students into college, but through college and into their desired career without a lifetime of debt. Success is predicated on a series of actions and decisions taken, starting today. If one fails to prepare, they are preparing to fail. Start making the right decision today by using this book as a tool on how to prepare, what steps to take, when to take them, how, and why.

Proper understanding of the content shared will lead you to a path of getting your child college and career ready starting in middle school and through their high school years. The key to this happening is by having a real plan. Then, you must work your plan daily because it won't happen by osmosis or without intentional actions. Let's get to work!

In an effort to reach the masses, this book was designed to speak to families at all levels, providing practical strategies that will empower parents with the right information to help your child become the driver of their own success, life, and become a unique person of value and significance. Again, our goal is to make what is a super complicated process easier to understand and navigate. College admissions and funding is a game. If you are unclear about the rules of engagement and how to play to win, it will swallow you up and put you on a path of debt. Know that there is a way out and a way to avoid this, and it starts with this book.

INTRODUCTION

"The time to be ready is never the time to start getting ready. If your desire is to win at life and to maximize every opportunity afforded, a position of staying ready is required."

THE COLLEGE PREP BOSS

You've certainly heard the phrase that our children are our future. But we must ask ourselves this: what kind of future are we setting them up to have or preparing them for? This is a question we must reflect upon and answer. Because here is the reality: the way we've been approaching the college admissions process is setting our kids up for starting life as an adult behind the starting line and playing catch up.

Taking an active and proactive role in facilitating their development before and during college is paramount to their success as an adult. The key to any amount of success, whether it's business, non-profit, or personal, is being grounded and having a strong foundation to build upon. This principle also applies to the development of our children. Their foundation is based on them having a strong educational backing. According to Webster Dictionary, there are several definitions for the word "foundation," but the following ones stick out the most:

1. the basis or groundwork of anything;
2. the natural or prepared ground or base on which some structure rests.

Now I'd like to bring to your attention the word "prepared." Having a foundation means that we have prepared the ground on which everything else stands. With a house, durability comes from building it on a solid rock. The foundation is the support of all other parts of the house and their ability to function properly. In addition, a solid foundation allows the house to be sturdy, so that it can stand the test of time. Just the same, by giving our children a solid educational and skill base, they will have the knowledge, confidence, and wisdom to navigate and compete in this world, as well as the ability to address and overcome obstacles they are sure to face.

Sadly enough, the country we live in spends more money on building jails and prisons than on educating our children–the ones who will help our country continue to thrive and exist. It is our responsibility to equip them because they, as well as the educational system itself, are in crisis, and it's beyond time to take action. We must own the educational process for our children and not rely solely on the system.

Because that educational system in the US is broken, a united partnership between families, the community, and the church is needed. Restoring the term "it takes a village" is needed now more than ever, to fill the familial, societal, and economic gaps and inequities that exist. This is especially true for communities of color. Everyone should be involved in the process of improving this situation.

If not, the following will continue to be the result, but on a higher level (as forecasted in *Jack Bennett's Opinion News*):

- "Nearly half of public assistance heads of family are dropouts. Dropouts are three times as likely to receive public assistance as graduates. (more welfare)

- Dropouts are 3.5 times as likely to be arrested as graduates. (more jails)

- Dropouts make up 82 percent of prison inmates. (more prisons)

- Dropouts earn less than one-third as much as graduates." (more welfare)

HOW TO MAXIMIZE USE OF THIS BOOK

There is so much to learn, process, and understand about college admissions, scholarships, and financial aid. Know that you are not alone. This book was created to help bring clarity to the chaos in a game not designed for you to win on your own.

In our Killing the College Game Program, we teach our proprietary system, which was built off what we call our College Admissions and Funding Formula: leadership, academics, community service, and test scores. Strategic implementation of this formula leads to a debt-free pathway. Now, don't get too excited because we won't get into the details of how our proprietary system works in this book; that is reserved for our VIP Clients. But what we will do is give you the baseline learning needed to understand how this system is applied and how it has helped our families accumulate over $40 million in scholarships. Simply put, it gives you the foundation for knowing how to play the game.

- So, in all your learning, gain a level of understanding by accomplishing the following objectives. You can further elevate your outcome by using the accompanying workbook and/or college planning journal.

- Get an understanding of how to monetize your scholar's skills and gifts and use it to select a viable career.

- Learn the art of setting and accomplishing practical goals, while driving accountability.

- Learn what and how to plan, and then work the plan daily to reach your defined level of success.

- Understand what college admissions is and what it requires.

- Learn the fundamental basics of financial aid and scholarships.

As in life, there are many paths one can take, and each path yields its own outcome. In this process, you will learn that there are many ways in which you can work toward achieving a higher education. There is no "one-size fits all," but there are fundamental basics, and this book will arm you with them. If you use it to craft a plan forward, you can be on a journey to a debt-free education. But it requires dedication, knowledge, a plan, and daily action.

First, read the book all the way through, take notes, set goals, and begin to create your own magic.

NEXT STEPS

Each chapter is designed to give you the fundamental basics that correspond with the exercises in the *College for Free Workbook* and *Debt Free College Planning Journal*. Using these books will help you formulate your own plan of attack. Of course, you can also opt to become a VIP Client, and we will craft your personalized strategy for you. Whether you are a do-it-yourself kind of family or you have us expertly coach you through it, do something. Your delay can cost your scholar tens of thousands of dollars and result in a lifetime of debt, also known as bondage.

Because this is a foreign concept to most families, we've included an Appendix and Glossary section to help translate the information shared in the chapters.

If you haven't yet realized this, your scholar must have a stake in this process. Schools, companies, and scholarship organizations are looking for students who exhibit strong leadership skills. With that said, please don't be the parent who wants to do all of this for their child. Have them learn the lesson of investing in their own growth and development, along with cultivating a work ethic and discipline for working for what they want, and not an ethic that says the world owes them something or they deserve it all because they have good grades. The process is much bigger than this.

Remember, you are getting them ready to compete globally while at the same time preparing them for post-secondary opportunities. Accomplish this by doing the following:

1. Become their development partner. Learn with them, help interpret what is learned and apply it.

2. Help them set short and long-term SMARTR goals (defined in next chapter).

3. Hold them accountable. Establish a system that facilitates check-ins, report outs, etc.

4. Monitor, measure, and track results. This allows you to examine when and where to modify your process and plan.

5. Incentivize the process. Motivate them by rewarding accomplishments, wins, and goal completion.

Now you are ready to go deeper and learn about the world of college admissions and funding.

CHAPTER 1
DEVELOPING A COLLEGE
& CAREER READY PLAN

"Those who succeed in life, do so because they plan & work it daily. Those who fail, fail because they fail to plan and, instead, rely on hope."

THE COLLEGE PREP BOSS

Has your child considered what the blueprint of their life should look like? Have they created a vision board that depicts who they want to be, where they want to go, what they want to have and who they want to be with? Well, they will soon have the tools for creating such a plan at the conclusion of this chapter. Their College and Career Ready Plan or, in simpler terms, their Life Plan, will serve as their blueprint for achieving their goals, visions, and aspirations. It will help them outline their goals, develop a plan of action for achieving them, and allow them to see where they will need to make changes, if necessary. The components of a life plan will vary depending on the person. For the stage they are at as a young person, here are some questions that apply to them:

✓   Where do you want to attend school?

✓   Where do you want to work?

✓ Where do you want to live?

✓ What career path do you want to follow after high school?

These questions can be intimidating or hard to think about all at once, but don't fret. The key to creating a plan and setting goals is to take it one step at a time. Once your child accomplishes small goals, they will eventually progress and tackle larger and more complex goals.

Ultimately, their post-secondary plan will get them focused and will help them to live a life on purpose and intentionally. By understanding who they are, what they want to do, and why they were created, they can then begin creating a plan that's based on serious thought and revelation. Getting in tune with their identity and purpose, as well as insight into a viable future path, will help them avoid feeling discouraged, disillusioned, wondering where they went wrong, feeling lost and misguided, or feeling worthless and wasting time.

WHY IS PLANNING IMPORTANT?

Usually, the first step in starting a business is creating a business plan. From there, businesses go on to develop strategic plans that focus on how to grow on a yearly basis, which outlines how they will be successful, produce a profit, and expand the business. Just as it is important in the business arena, it is equally crucial in one's personal life. Your child will apply the same principles.

They may be thinking to themselves that this is some heavy corporate stuff that is way over their head. They may be right. But know that the more knowledge they obtain now about how leaders think and operate, the more likely they will be able to compete globally at all levels. Plus, they are not too young to learn how to be global thinkers and leaders. It's all about college and career readiness. Colleges, universities, and scholarship agencies are seeking such leaders. It's all about how they can stand out and add value. To help ease their mind, let's look at something more practical.

We all like to go on vacation, right? So let's go! Your child is responsible for planning the family vacation six months from now. In order for all of you to have a relaxed and successful vacation, some planning must take place. Planning a successful vacation entails:

1. Determining a budget
2. Picking a destination
3. Selecting a travel time
4. Deciding on the type of vacation
5. Deciding if the family wants a resort, hotel, cruise, or condo
6. Checking for travel specials and deals on major travel sites
7. Research travel retailers and wholesalers for prices, ratings, amenities, etc.

8. Researching airline deals

9. Making reservations

10. Identifying items needed for the trip

11. Packing

12. Leaving for the trip

As you can see, everything is a process and steps are required to obtain success. Whether you are baking cookies, building a robot, creating a video game, or aiming to become valedictorian, it's all centered on a process of steps that are mapped out for execution. Taking it step by step helps to cover all bases, pay attention to detail, and ensure a successful delivery.

PLANNING FOR POST-SECONDARY SUCCESS

Let's translate this into life and, more specifically, getting into the college and career of their choosing. Have your young scholar answer the following questions: What are their intentions for their life? How do they plan to spend their time during and after their school matriculation? Do they plan to enter the military, travel, serve in another country with community service or mission organizations, start a business, attend college, or all of the above? Whatever the case is, it is important to have an idea of what they want to do in order to develop a successful plan of action that will bring their dreams to life.

Please know that their plans don't have to be an elaborate 5-page booklet, but it does need to be more detailed than, "I plan to travel a year around the world before going to school." They must outline what this year will look like: where they plan to go, how many places they will visit, what they will do while they are there, how they plan to fund this venture, what they plan to learn, and their next steps.

SETTING GOALS

A goal is a targeted objective intended to be achieved with a defined termination period. Goals provide clarity, direction, motivation, and focus.

People who write down specific goals for their future are far more likely to be successful than those who have either unwritten goals or no specific goals at all. The other part of their success is attributed to their ability to not only implement the plan they created, but to have the willpower to stick it out when the going gets tough. Achieving goals is not always a smooth path, as there are bound to be obstacles and roadblocks along the way.

Every successful person is a person of goals. Goals **must** be written. Only what is written down is remembered. Writing down their goals is the first act of commitment to themselves.

> "A man's private philosophy determines his public performance."
>
> BISHOP DALE BRONNER

I've heard my mentor and leaders say that you can tell the level of success a person will obtain when you review their daily agenda. Whatever you deem worthy of doing is worthy of being written down. When determining goals for your child's life, it is best to break them down into segments. This makes the goals easier to digest. The most common areas for which people write goals are:

- Career
- Personal
- Family
- Health
- Spiritual
- Friendship
- Community
- Education
- Financial
- Household
- Relationship

Once they categorize their goals, they must follow the SMARTR model:

S - Specific and Significant
M - Measurable, Motivational, Methodical & Meaningful
A - Action-Oriented and Achievable
R - Realistic
T - Time-Bound and Tangible
R - Relevant (to their mission/vision/purpose)

For the purpose of focusing on getting to college, they will set goals using the following categories, with the tools and options to include other areas as they go through the journey of life.

- Education
- Career
- Personal

Next, they will separate their goals in terms of short-term (1-90 days), mid-range (3-12 months), and long-range (1-5 years) goals.

Now, it's time to start setting some goals. Get a notebook, planner, or an app in your phone, and categorize each set of goals by type.

DEVELOPING A COLLEGE AND CAREER READY PLAN

Life plans are as unique as business plans are for organizations and companies. Based on the stage of life they are in, there are varying components. Sample areas of a life plan include:

- Core Values
- Purpose
- Dreams
- Family
- Employees
- Financial

- Friendships
- Fun
- Exit Plan
- Interests
- Location
- Physical Health
- Relationships
- Society/Community Involvement
- Church
- Professional/Career

For the sake of enforcing the learning in this chapter, they will create a life plan in line with what they have learned so far, and the information to follow. This will serve as a baseline for them to build upon as they advance in life. As life changes and evolves, so will their plan. It will forever be a living document. For now, their life plan will incorporate the following components:

1. Mission
2. Vision
3. Values Statement
4. Goals (Educational, Personal, Career)
5. Short-Term, Mid-Range, and Long-Term Goals
6. Accountability Partners (mentors, parents, coaches, etc.)

7. Potential Obstacles

8. Combat Tools

A life plan will help them establish consistency in their life; therefore, their life will be intentional and they will be positioned to win. It also creates a system, which has staying power and brings about order. Here are key steps to helping them remain consistent in this process:

1. Figure Out How To Do It

2. Write It Down

3. Practice It

4. Keep Improving It

5. Repeat the Process Cycle

Life planning sheets for each section can be found in the appendix, allowing them the opportunity to pull the information together into a working document.

MISSION STATEMENT

Writing their personal mission statement results in self-examination and requires them to know who they are. A personal mission statement is a brief description of the direction they want their life to go in, their area of focus, desired accomplishments, and aspirations. It enables them to FOCUS their life on a purposed course, eliminating the use of misappropriated energy and time.

F — First Things First (Forget About the Past)

O — Other Things Second

C — Cut the Unimportant (Stop Wasting Time)

U — Unify Their Vision

S — Stick With It

Personal mission statements are short-term in nature. They are created to capture their plans at a high level for the next one to three years.

VISION STATEMENT

Writing a vision means taking a picture of how they see the future, so they can identify how to focus now. A vision statement challenges students to capture a futuristic view of what they want to envision for their life in ten to fifteen years. It's not the same as the mission statement, but they should complement each other.

VALUES STATEMENT

Value statements are rooted in values and define how they conduct themselves with others, organizations, institutions, or families. Values are traits or qualities they hold in high regard; they serve as the driving forces of their existence. They serve as part of their moral fabric.

ACCOUNTABILITY PARTNERS

No one person can do anything by themselves. They will need someone to keep them on track, cheer them on, motivate them, and even chastise them. Therefore, it is important to think about who is in their life that they can trust to fill these shoes. It must be someone they respect and someone who will be frank, upfront, and honest with them. This person can be a parent, mentor, counselor, coach, or even a minister. I also suggest that they select someone currently working in the field they are interested in.

POTENTIAL OBSTACLES

Any person who plans effectively anticipates potential pitfalls and obstacles that may occur on their journey. It's the way to being an intentional leader. Granted, there will be situations they cannot plan for, but the ability to think forwardly will put them in a better position than someone who hasn't considered the possibility. So, as they process and think through their game plan, think about the things that can potentially go wrong and derail or delay their plans. Once they identify these challenges, think about ways they can overcome them and continue on their path. They will do this by asking themselves the following questions:

- ✓ Is there a viable alternative that can be executed?
- ✓ Is there someone I can reach out to who can assist me through this time?

✓ What am I supposed to learn from this challenge and how will it help me in the long run?

✓ Is there something I could have done differently to change the outcome?

✓ How does this goal fit into my master plan?

COMBAT TOOLS

Good soldiers are armed with tools to defend themselves and protect them from harm and danger. The same concept applies to life, business, school, and family. One must identify tools that will help them operate on a higher level than everyone else. They must also have the right attitude that is geared at succeeding and doing what it takes regardless of the sacrifice or challenge.

> *"Problems cannot be solved on the same level they were created."*
> ALBERT EINSTEIN

Here are some behavioral tools and principles they will need to help them weather the storms of life as they are in pursuit of their aspirations and dreams.

✓ Set goals and don't be afraid to adjust and adapt.

✓ Eliminate the excuses. Excuses keep them where they are and grant them permission to fail.

✓ Don't wait for something to happen, but rather initiate and take action. Be a solution–a change agent!

✓ Abstain from complaining. Make the best of every situation and find a way to convert the negative to a positive.

✓ Focus on what they are passionate about.

✓ Know that adversity and challenges are temporary.

✓ Have a support (dream) team.

✓ Have a "never give up" attitude.

BECOMING A WELL-ROUNDED STUDENT

This process is beyond just academics. How you are socially, professionally, emotionally, and academically presents a total being, not just one unbalanced side. Students setting themselves apart from other students require certain habits, behaviors, and even sacrifices. There will be times where they will have to decide whether they can go to the mall with their friends or if they will instead volunteer with a youth group because they made a commitment to be there. These types of decisions are part of growing up and being a leader.

John Maxwell, an expert on leadership and one of my mentors, has published a litany of books, one of them being *The 360° Leader*. Maxwell provides recipes for developing and maintaining effective relationships, leaders, and attitudes, as well as equipping individuals and organizations with crucial know-how. For the sake of developing leaders of today, tomorrow, and the future, we are going to adapt some of the basic principles he identifies as a necessity in order to stand out as a true leader in comparison to simply an average leader. In other words, he paints a picture of the kind of person who is desired by every company and organization. Remember, their goal is to get noticed, admitted, funded, and employed. With that in mind, these principles can be parlayed into the educational arena by teaching them the traits they need to attract the desire of every college and university. Possessing these virtues will endow them, as a student, with the edge they will need to thrive in academia, the community, and in professional settings. Let's identify what these principles are and set the stage for excelling in everything life has to offer.

- Adaptability—Quickly adjusts to change
- Discernment—Understands the real issues
- Perspective—Sees beyond their own vantage point
- Communication—Links to all levels
- Servanthood—Does whatever it takes
- Resourcefulness—Finds creative ways to make things happen
- Maturity—Puts the team before self
- Endurance—Remains consistent in character and competence over the long haul
- Countability—Can be counted on when it counts

Now that they know how to position themselves for greatness, it's time to put the principles into action and create a portfolio that exemplifies each area. Their portfolio will help them stay focused and intentional, while remaining true to their goals and aspirations. In addition, it can serve as a brag book when they pursue scholarship and job opportunities. Here are some examples of things they can do:

- Become an active volunteer or member of community organizations, nursing homes, youth centers, etc.

- Create a community focused organization that supports a disadvantaged population

- Go abroad and study in another country for the summer

- Participate in extracurricular activities and take on leadership positions, such as student government, Toastmasters, the science club, etc.

- Don't settle for mediocre. Take advanced, challenging, and unique courses, such as IB/AP courses, dual enroll at a college, debate, Japanese, Arabic, etc.

- Read and understand business publications, such as Wall Street Journal, Forbes, Black Enterprise, etc.

- Start or participate in an Investment Club

- Tutor and mentor other students

- Broaden their cultural awareness through music and arts by attending a symphony, opera, art exhibits, museums, etc.

- Participate in thought provoking activities or sports such as chess, golf, Cash Flow for Kids, etc.

- Enroll in IB/AP classes in high school and take the required test upon graduation. They can earn college credits upon passing the exam.

This will become the foundation for their life. You and your child should take the time to digest and process the information from this chapter. Take it to heart and begin the planning and development process by completing the corresponding pages in the Appendix.

The goal is to be a well-balanced student with strong demonstration of leadership, academic, and community service records. It speaks to who the student is as a person, leader, potential future alumnus, and member of the community. It also shows the student cares about others as well as themselves.

CHAPTER TAKEAWAYS

1. Key Learnings (what you didn't know before):

_____

_____

_____

_____

2. What You Need to Unlearn or Stop Doing:

_____

_____

_____

_____

3. What You Need to Do Next:

_____

_____

_____

_____

CHAPTER 2
CHOOSING THE RIGHT CAREER

"The point of life is not to slave away for years until the age of 65 and then say 'Phew, glad that's over!' Rather, it is to make sure that we do not die with our music still in us."

LANCE SECRETAN

Median Earnings by Education Level and Age, 2013–2017

Age	High School Diploma	Some College, No Degree	Associate Degree	Bachelor's Degree
18	$18,600	$0	$0	$0
19	$18,600	$16,600	$0	$0
20	$22,600	$23,000	$25,600	$0
21	$22,600	$23,000	$25,600	$0
22 to 24	$22,600	$23,000	$25,600	$35,400
25 to 29	$29,300	$31,400	$35,400	$46,000
30 to 34	$31,900	$37,100	$41,200	$55,200
35 to 39	$36,300	$41,900	$46,600	$65,700
40 to 44	$37,300	$45,500	$49,500	$70,800
45 to 49	$40,100	$47,800	$51,800	$74,300
50 to 54	$41,200	$49,400	$52,300	$75,800
55 to 59	$41,200	$49,600	$52,600	$73,600
60 to 64	$40,400	$49,300	$52,300	$70,000

SOURCE: THE COLLEGEBOARD & U.S. CENSUS BUREAU

Selecting a career choice or vocation is one of the most important decisions a student will make in their life. It will set the foundation for how their life progresses and the opportunities that will be afforded to them. An important factor in selecting an area of study is to align their decision with something they are passionate about. They never want to make a decision based solely on its monetary value, but base it also on their interests, vision, goals, skills, and passion. As a result, they will be one step closer toward a purpose-driven life—a life that gives them more value, career satisfaction, a sense of accomplishment, and a higher level of achievement. Furthermore, selecting a career path based on this type of data minimizes the chance of changing their major. According to the National Center for Education Statistics, "within three years of initial enrollment, about 30 percent of undergraduates in associate's and bachelor's degree programs who had declared a major had changed their major at least once." This means that approximately one-third of all college students changed course during their academic careers. Within this number, 1 in 10 changed their major more than once. Every time a student changes their major, it oftentimes leads to more time added to the clock, and that translates into more money, more money.

To set them on the path of living a life of intentionality and purpose, we are going to journey through the following stages toward ascertaining a definite career path by focusing only on interest and skills.

Stage 1: Identify Interest and Gifts
Stage 2: Align Interests with Career Fields
Stage 3: Research and Finalize Career Field
Stage 4: Identify Steps for Pursuing Career Field
Stage 5: Take Action

"Talent alone will not make you a success. Neither will being at the right place at the right time, unless you are ready. The important question is, 'Are you ready?'"

JOHNNY CARSON

The Bureau of Labor Statistics reports that men and women hold an average of about 14 jobs by the time they turn 40. Kelly Services, a major temporary staffing agency, reports that almost half of adults are not completely satisfied with the requirements, lack of flexibility, risks, and compensation of their current jobs. Many of these individuals will consider changing careers. A recent study published by Best Colleges reported that 61% of college grads would change their majors if they could turn back time. Our goal is to prevent this from happening. We want your child to make an informed decision because they did the research and took the experiential step on the front ends. Let's take a look at the stages to selecting the right career path.

STAGE 1: IDENTIFY INTEREST AND GIFTS

The key to career satisfaction is to find an occupation that they can enjoy and excel in at the same time. This can be achieved by matching both their abilities and interests to their desired career field. I would dare them to take it a step further by encouraging them to understand what their purpose is. Understanding why they were created is a fundamental piece of the puzzle of existence as it relates to living a full life.

For the sake of this section, we are going to focus on their interests and abilities.

1. Who am I?
2. What do I like to do?
3. What are my hobbies?
4. What am I good at?

The above are some initial questions they can ask themselves to begin the process. If they never thought about the answers to these questions, that is okay. We are going to explore them and many more on a quest to determine who they are by answering a Career Interest and Career Skills Questionnaire. They will find many personality and skills assessment sites that are free and great at aligning their abilities with potential career fields.

- Interests are defined as things they are passionate about and feel called to take part in. Examples include ballet, basketball, arcade games, or teaching English to foreign students.

- Skills are things that they are able to do well, such as writing articles, working on car engines, shooting three pointers, or giving speeches.

Once they narrow down who they are, what they like to do, and the skills they possess, they are ready to move on to the next step and review possible career choices and narrow them down to a final choice.

STAGE 2: ALIGN INTERESTS WITH CAREER FIELDS

Matching their interests and skills/talents with possible careers must happen naturally. Everyone is born with natural gifts and talents that give them the ability to complete special assignments in their life that benefit others.

They will use their results from the questionnaires they completed and narrow down the potential careers that best suit them. Ideally, they will select the top four career possibilities where they scored the highest. These will be the top areas that are more in line with what matters most to them and their skill level. From here, they will further review the careers, examine the career options, and select the ones that interest them the most. Of all the options, select the ten occupations they are compelled to learn more about.

Keep in mind there is no perfect process for selecting the right career, as there is a chance they can end up with a job that will not incorporate all their interests or use all their skills. At the same time, having this information and completing the process will ensure they are better equipped and educated to make this important decision.

STAGE 3: RESEARCH AND FINALIZE CAREER FIELD

This stage is about decreasing that potential list of ten to no more than three career choices. They will arrive at this list by investigating the fields and creating a list of things that attract them, as well as listing the characteristics that are not so attractive. Then they will review the commitments required for each field (work schedule, travel requirements, minimum work hours per week, holidays, etc.) and decide if this aligns with their vision for their life.

After answering these questions, they should be able to pare down their list and make a final selection.

Another point to consider in view of a career field: what is the demand for this field in the next ten to twenty years? Will there be jobs available? The following resources and options are available to answer these questions:

- Interviewing family, friends, and others
- Internet
- *Occupational Outlook Handbook* website
- Library
- Career centers
- Trade and business publications
- Seminars, trainings, clubs, trade shows, or conferences
- Networking and mentors

STAGE 4: IDENTIFY STEPS FOR PURSUING CAREER FIELD

Now that a decision has been made regarding the preferred career of choice, they will need to know what is required to pursue this profession. Are there certain skills required that they lack, such as four years of Latin, the completion of physics, calculus, and computer programming? Do they need to have three years of working as an intern or in co-op?

Or do they need to have 100 hours of live video production time completed with ten finished projects? Questions like these will help them map out a plan of execution for bringing their desired career into fruition. They can obtain this information by checking out the resources outlined above, along with speaking to a guidance counselor or mentor, by visiting universities or trade schools, and by conducting informational interviews with professionals in the field along with professional organizations.

STAGE 5: TAKE ACTION

They have taken a major step in learning more about who they are and what they have to offer, while discovering how to apply that to a real-life decision of selecting a career. It's now time to bring the information to reality. Take action and get moving!

The final component of execution is to look for opportunities to volunteer in order to get real life experience working in the field. This will give them valuable insight of what they can expect as far as expectations and potential challenges, and can minimize the number of misconceptions and unrealistic truths. Finding these opportunities can come by networking with professionals and professional organizations. Remember: an answer to a problem is always a person. Therefore, it is important to engage themselves with a good mentor and to network with people aspiring after the same thing and who are where they want to be. Choose wisely, because there are four types of people that exist in this life:

1. People who add to you

2. People who subtract from you

3. People who multiply you

4. People who divide you

It is their choice on the type of people they allow to consume their time, energy, and gifts and take up valuable space in what we call their "inner circle." You have to help them make the best decision.

> *"There are some people who live in a dream world, and there are some who face reality; and then there are those who turn one into the other."*

DOUGLAS EVERETT

CHAPTER TAKEAWAYS

1. **Key Learnings (what you didn't know before):**

_____

_____

_____

_____

2. What You Need to Unlearn or Stop Doing:

_____

_____

_____

_____

3. What You Need to Do Next:

_____

_____

_____

_____

CHAPTER 3
CHOOSING THE RIGHT SCHOOL

"If you educate a man you educate a person, but if you educate a woman, you educate a family."

RUDY MANIKAN

Choosing a school can be a stressful decision and process, especially with the high levels of student loan debt in this country and unsteady job market. There are many questions running through students' heads, and in your minds as parents, as well. You are likely afraid of the unknown: affordability, social lifestyle, safety, quality of education, how to get there, and even if you will survive. Let me put your mind at ease because this chapter will help you answer all these questions and so much more. Let's first start with understanding the types of schools that exist.

Because colleges are not a "one size fits all" model, there are several different types of schools you can attend based on career interest, class size, financial ability, and an ongoing list of classifications. In terms of the type of school, you basically have the following in the list below.

Elite schools have the most restrictive admission criteria. They consist of about 70 schools and have the following characteristics:

- Highly Competitive – they accept fewer than 30% of applicants. You require a high GPA, stellar test scores, superior writing abilities, and a solid record of extracurricular achievement

- Often Diverse - they can control the makeup of their student body since they receive more applicants than they accept. Students tend to come from all walks of life: upper, middle, and lower economic classes, various cultures, races, and nationalities

- Higher Quality of Education – with high tuition, large endowments, and many federal grants, the school has the affordability to spend top dollar for top notch professors, along with having the latest equipment and facilities. Most keep class sizes down and insist on meaningful student-faculty interaction

- Attract Top-Notch People - they draw the best faculty, students, and staff in the business

- Have Large Endowment Funds – they have stronger ability to offer merit scholarships to qualified students and drastically decrease the large price tag for a quality education

Elite schools are often referred to as Ivy League schools, but there is also another group of schools classified as Public Ivies and "The Other" Elites. Here are some examples of each group:

The Ivy League consists of the following eight schools:

Brown University

Columbia University

Cornell University

Dartmouth College

Harvard University

Princeton University

University of Pennsylvania

Yale University

The Public Ivies are public universities that are among the nation's most competitive schools, and include:

College of William and Mary

State University of New York at Binghamton

University of California, Berkeley

University of California, Los Angeles

University of Florida

University of Michigan

University of North Carolina

University of Virginia

University of Washington

University of Wisconsin, Madison

Public Ivies are great choices for students who want to attend a highly selective college with state-of-the-art facilities and world class instruction, but can't pony up a small fortune in tuition.

The Other Elites are hard-to-classify elites that are extremely competitive, offer outstanding academic programs, and attract the best and most talented students and faculty.

Bowdoin College

Davidson College in NC

Duke

George Washington University

Juilliard

Macalester College in MN

Massachusetts Institute of Technology (MIT)

Notre Dame

Stanford

United States Military Academy

Vanderbilt

Washington University in MO

Wesleyan University

State schools are part of the university system, are largely funded by tax dollars, and charge considerably less tuition than most private schools. Since they are usually large schools, they have many resources in terms of facilities and personnel. State schools have the following characteristics:

- Big - they can resemble a small city, with thousands of students, teachers, staff, and hundreds of academic disciplines. Everything is oversized, including lecture halls, football games, dances, etc.

- Vary in selectivity - getting into a top state school outside a student's home state can be challenging because out-of-state enrollment is limited

- Serious resources - they offer just about every class you can imagine, along with access to state-of-the-art facilities

- Affordable - unless you come from out of state, public universities and colleges offer some of the best deals in higher education

Within the university system, there is usually a flagship school, which is usually the biggest, most prestigious, and most selective branch of the university. Based on the size of these institutions, the university system may divide them into smaller entities, identified as colleges. Flagships, along with state university systems, may also have branch locations across the city and state.

Historically Black Colleges & Universities (HBCU) provide a tight-knit environment that fosters education and a drive for success. These schools can be private, public, or liberal arts schools and are attended mostly by African American students.

Liberal Arts Schools believe that students should work closely with their teachers and should develop critical learning skills as well as intellectual curiosity. Some liberal arts colleges don't have majors or grades, but they do have requirements.

These schools have the following characteristics:

- Personal attention - small classes and attentive professors. They emphasize the importance of developing solid speaking and writing skills. You will not find large lecture halls, endless multiple choice exams, or teaching assistants.

- Very selective - there are more than 223 liberal arts colleges in the US (US News) and they can be among the most selective schools in the country. They also tend to have higher acceptance rates.

- Great education - they attract the brightest professors and staff in the world. These schools focus more on teaching and not on publishing compared to large universities. As well, students' thoughts and opinions tend to carry more value.

Most liberal arts colleges are private, but there are some that offer public school prices such as Truman State University, Ramapo College, and Sonoma State University. The public schools have such great reputations that they attract a large number of out-of-state students. Then you have liberal arts colleges that exist within public universities, which give students access to university resources, along with the added benefits of smaller class sizes and closer interaction with faculty and other students.

Two-Year Schools have a diverse student body and smaller class sizes. This group includes community and technical colleges, some of which offer four-year degrees.

These schools tend to attract students interested in taking classes only, rather than living in a dorm and participating in the social activities. Many students attend as a means to save money, and this sometimes serves as a pit stop on their way to a four-year university. Characteristics of two-year schools are:

- Not necessarily small - one of the largest colleges in the nation, Miami Dade Community College, has an enrollment of about 160,000 students

- Accepting - they admit the majority of their applicants. Typically, you will only need a high school diploma or a GED, as they don't usually require an ACT or SAT score. They generally, however, administer assessments to determine class placement

- Affordable – they have significantly less tuition than a public four-year college

- Lack of personalization - these are usually commuter schools, so they rarely offer dormitories and extensive student services

Community colleges are often referred to as Junior Colleges and they primarily offer Associate of Arts (AA) and Associate of Applied Science (AAS) degrees in a wide variety of fields.

Technical colleges focus primarily on providing specialized skills that will enable students to enter the workforce in lieu of pursuing a four-year degree. Most schools offer a wide range of programs, along with awarding

Associate of Technical Arts (ATA) and Associate of Applied Science (AAS) degrees. In finding a technical school, select one with programs that assist with placement into internships or apprenticeships during school matriculation and have a solid reputation for job placement.

Although a degree can be obtained from both types of colleges and can be transferred to a four-year institution, it is recommended to find schools with articulation agreements. This means that the school has contracts with four-year schools that specify which degrees and credits will transfer. You're absolutely looking for a program that will allow you to transfer all their credits. Also note that there is a level of difficulty in transferring to highly competitive schools. Therefore, it is important to be aware of their education plan and allowable concessions prior to enrolling.

Specialty schools include trade and proprietary schools that are private, for-profit institutions where students enroll to learn a practical skill required for entry into the workforce. Some of these schools offer both a Bachelor's and Master's degree. Characteristics of these schools include:

- Focused on learning - they don't offer many student activities, dormitories or sports. Class sizes are fairly small and can be even smaller at liberal arts college

- Pricey – they cost more than community and technical colleges and are not likely to offer any federal financial aid

- Accepting - they rarely turn away students

- Career-oriented – they are good choices if you decide to go directly into the workforce, but not so ideal if you decide to transfer to another school. Credits are difficult to transfer

Proprietary schools follow the demands and trends of the workforce, in which they quickly assemble educational programs to match.

Trade schools focus more on one specific field and offer hands-on training. Some popular examples of trade schools include culinary arts, flight, and cosmetology schools. Because of the specific licensure requirements for certain trades according to state regulations, it is critical for you to ensure the school offers the necessary information in their educational program.

Distance Learning Schools are in a bit of a league of their own. With constant advancement in technology as it relates to web interface and communication, more and more schools have embraced this phenomenon and now offer distance learning programs. Response from students has been high, so colleges are now offering the majority of their programs via online delivery methods. If you choose to go this route, be sure to research and check their accreditation as a way of avoiding fraudulent programs and illegitimate schools. Characteristics of distance learning schools include:

- Convenient – they are ideal for working adults and students in remote areas of the country

- Accepting - they admit almost anyone who can pay the tuition

- Reputable - a few of the larger schools have regional accreditation to offer legitimate degrees, and their students qualify for federal student aid. Some of the more reputable programs have articulation agreements with traditional college campuses so students can transfer credits or degrees

- Not always disembodied - many traditional campuses

- Also offer degrees online, giving students the convenience of distance learning but with the legitimacy of a traditional school if you are concerned an employer will not take these schools' degrees seriously

THE IMPORTANCE OF ACCREDITATION

You have likely heard the term "accreditation" during your child's educational tenure, but perhaps lack the understanding of its relevancy. Accreditation is basically a set of guidelines and criteria that schools go through in order to confer legitimate diplomas and degrees for educational completion. The accreditation process is managed and granted by approved agencies and is governed by the National Education Association.

This is important for several reasons. Firstly, corporations check to see if diploma holders come from an actual, accredited university and not a fake or low-quality school where almost anybody can get a diploma. Secondly, if you decide to pursue an advanced degree, colleges will turn you down for admission due to a lack of accredited class completion. As a result, you may be forced to repeat classes and spend more money.

You can validate a school's accreditation by requesting to see their credentials in writing and by checking the proper government agencies or the NEA.

FINDING THE BEST SCHOOL

There is plenty of information in books and on the internet to guide you on how to find the best school for your child's college career. You may not realize this, but it can actually be a simple process. After you decide on the type of school you would like to attend and you determine a field of study, you will then need to assess what is most important to you and select a school that can provide those things. Now don't get me wrong: college rankings according to US News, USA Education Guides, and Princeton Review are equally important and serve as a valuable source of information. This information should be used after you complete an internal assessment measuring their personal feelings, needs, beliefs, interests, and requirements. Here are some questions you can give your child to ask themselves to help determine the best school for them:

1. Do I want to go out of state? If yes, how far do I want to go?

2. Do I want a school that provides personalized teaching settings (smaller class sizes) or a school with larger classroom settings?

3. Do I want to attend a one gender school?

4. Is it necessary for me to attend graduate school? Do I want a five or six-year program that gives me a bachelors and masters?

5. What social activities am I interested in (Greek-Life, student government, intramural sports, etc.)?

6. Do I want to go to school in a small town or in a metropolitan city?

7. I am a sports fan, so do I want a school with a big athletic program?

8. Do I have a strong, average, or weak academic profile?

Now that you have challenged your child with some questions to ascertain what they require to have a successful college life, you can look at college rankings by various categories to assist you in the final decision. Some of the ranking categories include:

- Best college or university in the USA by major
- Best college or university in the USA by location
- Best college or university in the USA by school type

Please note that these rankings are not the gospel. They provide insightful information, but you must decide what school is the best fit socially, academically, emotionally, financially, and professionally for your child.

MAKING THE CUT

There is no limit on the number of schools you can apply for. But keep in mind the fact that each application requires time, energy, and money. It is best that you narrow their list down to a manageable number of about six schools (minimum). You can accomplish this by:

- ✓ Talking to friends and family: these will be people you highly respect, preferably graduates of the schools you are interested in

- ✓ Talking to their guidance counselor: they have valuable input to aid you in your child's decision, along with assisting you with their transcripts, recommendations, and other essentials needed for the application

- ✓ Listing their criteria: imagine their ideal school and list what it would look like in terms of academics, location, size, sports, student body, and so on

- ✓ Attending college fairs: identify local fairs at their school, community organizations or local universities and attend so you can speak to college reps and receive brochures and information.

- ✓ Requesting school information: go online or call the admissions office to make a request, and also ask for financial aid info

✓ Refine their choices: divide the list into three categories - dream, target and safe schools

✓ Stay organized: create a system for tracking the schools you are interested in pursuing

The final action item to aid you in finalizing this decision is the campus visit. Because this can be an expensive task, it is recommended that you conduct visits in your child's sophomore year at least. There are several ways to approach these visits. One way is to target only the schools you are interested in pursuing. Another method is to visit several schools in each category (private, state, specialty, etc.). Then again, you can approach visits geographically by visiting schools by regions, states, or cities. It is their decision, but I cannot stress enough the amount of time and money that goes into campus visits. Yet, clearly and also advantageously, it is a necessity. Here are some tips to help you with scheduling college visits:

✓ Check the school's schedule: make sure the college is in session and see if they have special times allocated for visits

✓ Schedule engagements: contact the admissions office and request to sit in on a class or two. Interview professors, interview students, setup a meeting with financial aid and the dean of the college of interest

✓ Be prepared: be on time for these appointments, have a plan for the visit, and dress neatly. Not necessarily in a suit, but be presentable

✓ Explore the campus: someone from the admissions office or a student guide will probably take you on a tour, but be prepared to tour the campus independently, meet people, and get a real feel of the environment

✓ Stay the night: consider asking to spend the night in a dorm to gain a genuine experience of campus life

✓ Go off-campus: visit the surrounding areas of the campus, explore the town or city, and identify what is close by like apartments, shopping areas, bookstores, the airport, etc.

✓ Take notes: write down their observations, thoughts, and mental notes about the visit

✓ Send "thank you" notes: after returning home, write and send notes of appreciation to all the individuals you met and talked to on the academic staff and faculty. Remain in contact with those you connect with, and continue to expand this network

HOW DO I GET THERE: THE APPLICATION PROCESS?

Applying for college is best done online. You can access a college application by either going to the desired school's website or to one of the college application consortium websites.

- Common Application: www.commonapp.org

- Universal College Application: www.universalcollegeapp.com

- HBCU Common Application: http://commonblackcollegeapp.com/

- The Coalition: www.coalitionforcollegeaccess.org

- If you require a paper copy, contact the admissions office and request an application packet. Here are some key pointers in completing the application:

- Fill out the application as legibly as possible using a black or blue ink pen if an online application is not available

- Allow enough time to complete the application process. Start as early as possible.

- Be aware of all deadlines, requirements, tests, recommendations, etc.

In addition, below are some basic helpful guidelines when completing the application. Make sure that you equip your child with this list and have them follow it closely.

What To Do:

- ✓ Read application directions carefully.

- ✓ Create an application checklist per school.

- ✓ Make sure everything that is supposed to be included is enclosed.

✓ your applications yourself. Type the information personally to avoid crucial mistakes.

✓ Create a system that starts with the simplest application, then progress to the more complicated ones.

✓ Create a practice application per school to work from, then transfer final details to the real application upon completion.

✓ Type clear answers and then proofread the applications and essays several times for accuracy. Also, ask someone else to proofread them for you.

✓ Always *describe* how you can make a contribution to the schools vs. *telling* them.

✓ Be truthful, and do not exaggerate accomplishments.

✓ Keep a copy of all forms you submit to colleges. There's always a chance you will have to resubmit information.

✓ Be thorough and always meet your deadlines.

What Not To Do:

• Leave blank spaces. Missing information can lead to a delay in processing your application and having it possibly disqualified or rejected

- Send in an incomplete package. Just like blank spaces, missing files requested by the school can delay the process or lead to a rejected application.

- Be ambiguous and vague. Don't deflect and provide a response or details that do not answer the question in its entirety.

- Have a third-party complete your application for you. You must own this process from beginning to end, and that includes the content. When having it completed by others, you can't honestly verify that what is shared is accurate and true. Falsified information will hurt you in the long run, even after you start your program.

- Put it off! Timing is everything. Delays in the process can cost you opportunities.

The application package has two components: the student portion and the high school portion. You'll complete the student section and submit it to the respective college or university. The school section will be sent directly from the school, and it usually covers transcript information, a counselor statement, secondary school report, and teacher evaluation forms.

Another part of the student section is the college admission essay and, sometimes, an entrance interview.

- Admissions essays serve as your child's voice and a way for the selection committee to get to know you beyond the numbers. Be sure to read the questions carefully and follow directions. It is important for you to brainstorm ideas, create rough drafts, proofread, and have several other people read their essay. Highlight their achievements and those characteristics that make them special, unique, and deserving of admission.

- Interviews are not always required, but they serve as another way for the committee to get to know the student. Verify with the schools of interest to see if they offer interviews. If they are part of the process, your child should be prepared to articulate who they are in a conversational-type environment. Then have a list of questions ready to ask the admissions representative. Also be prepared technologically, because some schools conduct interviews using Zoom, Microsoft Teams, and other platforms.

The college admission essay can be on a variety of topics. Some may ask one specific question, while others may ask you to choose three topics from a longer list of questions. On the other hand, the school may not list any topics and allow your child to freestyle with their writing. In any event, the scenario can vary from school to school. Your child just needs to be prepared to cover the basics of writing: grammar, spelling, tense shifts, subject/verb agreement, passive voice, wordiness, and punctuation. The essay can make or break the admissions process, and a strong academic portfolio and a poor essay could impede chances of acceptance.

It is crucial to be mindful of the quality of the essay. Here are eight of the most common types of questions:

1. Choose a significant experience you have had, achievement you have attained, risk you have taken, or ethical dilemma you have faced, and discuss its impact on you.

2. Examining your local and global environment, share the issues that concern you the most? These issues can be personal, community, nationwide, or global.

3. Describe a situation or someone who has had a significant influence on you, and explain what that influence has been.

4. Describe a character in fiction, a historical figure, or a creative work (art, music, film, etc.) that has had an important influence on you, and explain that influence.

5. Our campus is enriched by the wide range of our students' academic interests, personal perspectives, and life experiences. Diversity at many levels is a hot discussion. Please describe a personal experience that illustrates what you would bring to the diversity of a college community, or a diversity-related situation that impacted you or is of great importance to you.

6. Explain something you have failed in, how it affected you, what you learned, and how you bounced back.

7. Explain a difficult situation or a class you were struggling in where you had to find a way to overcome. How did you go about overcoming? What did you learn from it?

8. COVID has impacted many in a variety of ways. Share how COVID made you better or prompted you to make life better for others?

These questions can be used to brainstorm and think through ways to articulate how you process the issues and challenges of life, how you lead and solve problems, etc. Your ability to express yourself adds dimension to what's on your application. In an era where communication and soft skills are critical, the quality of a student's essay can make or break their application.

Being proactive and practicing what to say, how to say it, and how to frame it is essential in this process. So much is at stake and this part of the process cannot be taken lightly. The goal here is to prepare you to conquer the essay section and minimize anxiety or writer's block while demonstrating how you would add value to that institution.

When writing a sound essay or paper, it is built using the same framework: introduction, body, and conclusion. But understand that college and scholarship essays are very different from academic writing. You will always need a thesis as the central point of the essay, but the essay should demonstrate and illustrate your thoughts creatively with a persuasive tone.

Below are a few sample structures that can be used to write and format the essays needed for admissions and scholarships.

- Chronological Structure – these types of essays work forward in time. Their thesis paragraph may start at a dramatic moment, after which the first body paragraph may double back to begin at the beginning.

- Half & Half – this type describes a cause-and-effect or a before-and-after relationship. The first half will either focus on the cause or on what you were like before an experience, event, or encounter. The second half will focus on either the effect or on what you were like afterward. The key here is to not focus on describing the experience, event, or encounter, but on you and your viewpoints.

- The Three Elements - this is similar to the standard essay structure. Instead of presenting arguments and supporting paragraphs, you will describe each point in detail that illustrates who you are.

Last, but not least, here are some essential rules for your child to keep in mind when writing the essay:

- Be a little self-centered. This will be one of the few opportunities they will have to brag and talk about themselves, so they need to take advantage of the situation. The committee wants to know who they are, what they've accomplished, what impact they have made in the lives of others, and where they come from.

- Be specific. Avoiding vague phrases and clichés is key Providing clear and concise details and minimizing the fluff talk always makes for a sound essay

- Be aware of the rest of their application. Make sure their essay is consistent with the other parts of their application. Highlight the areas that are not emphasized.

- Be funny and creative, but be careful. Use genuine, but respectful humor. It can add punch to their essay and show that they are smart and human. Showing creativity in their approach can make their essay memorable and impactful.

- Be focused. Do not ramble and appear unfocused. Although creativity is warranted, they must make sure the objective is met and the question is answered. The ultimate goal is to show the admissions officers why they would be a valuable member of their school's academic community.

- Hook them in the first few sentences. It's like reading a good book. If it doesn't catch your attention in the beginning, it will be difficult to continue. Using creativity, find a way to hook them in the beginning and then keep their interest to continue reading.

- Show their personality and be authentic. Admissions officers want to know the student applying to their school. Convey the message in a relatable fashion that tells the audience who your child really is.

- Have a strong close. You never want to leave the reader hanging by getting them hooked at the beginning and not maintaining the storyline or connecting the dots all the way to the end.

The best way to prepare for the student section and the application process is to prepare a student resume or record of achievement. This is basically their academic portfolio that will be deemed valuable not only during the application process itself, but also for the scholarship application process. It's what I call their scholarship portfolio, which is a "brag sheet" in plain English. Their resume should include:

- Grade point average

- Honor courses taken

- AP or IB courses taken

- Standardized test scores

- Special talents

- Academic awards received

- Sports accomplishments

- Extracurricular activities and any positions held

- Organizations or community initiatives they started, implemented, and executed
- Community service
- Completed college courses
- College goals

With social media and technology, there are creative ways to build your college ready resume. You can either search for online portfolio tools or create a LinkedIn account. If you're not aware. LinkedIn is a social media platform for professionals, but it has expanded its audience to include high school students, colleges, and universities. Remember, the goal is to be college and career ready, and therefore LinkedIn is an awesome choice. Also, it increases visibility to colleges, admissions representatives, companies, and so on. It can play into short and long term career goals.

The admissions interview is not always required by schools. If they do require it, it may take place on or off campus with an admissions representative, an alum or a student, and in person or virtually through the use of technology. Interviews can be stressful and nerve racking, but you can overcome this by preparing and practicing. Here are some tips for your child to relieve the stress of the interview process:

✓ Prepare, but don't memorize - Think about possible questions and how you might respond beforehand. Practice answering as many questions as you can.

You will find sample questions in the appendix. Don't commit speeches to memory.

✓ Dress nicely - You will want to appear professional with a nice business suit or pantsuit in neutral colors (black, navy blue, grey, or brown). A three-piece suit or a prom dress is a bit overboard, and flip flops, hoodies, jeans, shorts, caps, T-shirts, and giant earrings are forbidden.

✓ Good hygiene - Wash, brush, floss, pluck, shave, and deodorize. Go easy on the makeup and fragrances. Do not chew gum.

✓ Strike the right tone - Be confident, but not cocky or arrogant. You want to be open and genuine, but not inappropriate or rude. No profanity, slang, or improper language. Maintain this same presence when you speak to kids on the campus.

✓ Provide substantial answers - Do not mumble or provide closed-ended answers like "yes" or "no," or have a long lapse of silence. Be conversational and have thorough answers when responding to questions.

✓ Explain - Be prepared to explain any negative or concerning marks on the application, transcripts, or with test scores without appearing as if you're whining or making excuses. Make sure the explanations are reasonable and sound.

✓ Ask questions - You will most definitely be asked by the official at the end of the interview if you have any questions for them. "Uh" and "I don't think so," are not the right answers. See sample questions in the appendix.

✓ Have examples of leadership, lessons learned, overcoming identified and ready to share.

✓ Get educated on the school – What are notable facts about the school? Have they been in the news lately?

The interview is not a one-way process, but a two-way experience. It is an opportunity for you to learn more about the school and determine if it is a good fit or not, while selling yourself to the admissions officer. Let them see your leadership qualities shine in the interview and be excited about admitting you to their institution.

AUDITIONS AND PORTFOLIOS

If you plan to pursue the arts, music or theater fields, in addition to the school band, cheerleading or dance team, you may be required to audition and/or provide a portfolio to the admissions personnel and more than likely to the departmental representative. The following tips and suggestions will help you effectively prepare and show themselves in the best light possible when going through the audition and portfolio process.

MUSIC AUDITIONS

Students who wish to pursue a degree in music, whether vocal or instrumental, typically must audition. If you're a singer, prepare at least two pieces in contrasting styles. A good way to distinguish yourself is to perform a piece in a foreign language, if possible. Then make your selection from operatic, show music, or art song repertories, and make sure you memorize each piece. If you're an instrumentalist or pianist, be prepared to play scales and arpeggios, at least one etude or technical study, and a solo work. Instrumental audition pieces need not be memorized. In either field, be prepared, ready and able to do sight-reading.

When performing music that is sight-read, take time to look over the piece and make certain of the key and time signatures before proceeding with the audition. If you're a singer, you should bring a familiar accompanist to the audition. Seek the advice of teachers and other students in the department and, if possible, to try to acquire audition information up front and in advance. A great rule of thumb is to know more than is required for the audition and select the audition time and date early.

Practice, practice, and practice is critical to the preparation phase. Practice their piece in front of a diverse audience and various times. After each practice performance, seek detailed feedback regarding their delivery, articulation, tone, and overall performance. Another way to prepare is to audition and participate in as many performances as possible.

Because programs differ, it is recommended that students contact the college for audition information. In general, music departments seek students who demonstrate technical competence and performance achievement.

Admission to music programs vary in degree of competitiveness, so you should audition at multiple schools, around three to five schools. This will increase your chance of admittance. The degree of competitiveness varies also by instrument, especially if a renowned musician teaches a certain instrument. Some colleges offer a second audition if you feel you did not audition to their potential. Therefore, be sure to ask if this is offered at your schools of choice. Ideally, being accepted by the top choice of school is always the goal, but unfortunately that may not be the case and you will need to have a contingency plan. You will need to make the decision to either pursue a music program at another college or consider another major at that college.

DANCE AUDITIONS

The approach will vary, but a common format will include colleges having an open-call day or a technique class. This day gives aspiring dancers the opportunity to learn about the varying techniques and styles they will be expected to demonstrate in their audition and showcase their level of awareness and ability to interact with other dancers. It would be a good idea to research the school for insight in this area. At minimum, be prepared to showcase the following individually and collectively: ballet, modern, and maybe jazz. Those assessing the auditions look for students to display a level of competence in coordination, technique, rhythm, degree of movement, and body structure. The dance faculty members will also rate the students' ability to learn, and their potential to complete the curriculum. Just like with music auditions, dance programs vary, so the need to check with the college of their choice for specific information is necessary. You should also consider the advice and consultation of area dance professionals familiar with the process. Your goal is to shine and excel with your techniques, improvisation, and solos.

Band, drill-team, dance team, and cheerleading all require auditions and have the same basic principles as outlined for music and dance auditions above. Applicants will be assessed based on their level of competence, technique, coordination, and rhythm. The best approach is to have a video portfolio of their performances ready to display and present to the school representatives. Then, contact the school to request information concerning requirements, the audition process, and auditions dates.

ART PORTFOLIOS

A portfolio is basically a compilation of their presentable artwork. When selecting art pieces to include in their portfolio, you should demonstrate their interest and aptitude for a serious education in the arts. Focusing on these areas and providing the necessary attention in assembling such a package will position your child to receive scholarships and compete in national portfolio competitions. Also, be sure their selected pieces show diversity in technique and variety in the subject matter covered. You are given the liberty to showcase any medium: oils, pastels, photography, in black and white or color. Please note that their portfolio is not limited to any group of work, but open to any creations you have: classroom, personal drawings, independent projects, etc.

Specialized art colleges typically request applicants to present about ten pieces of art, but keep in mind the focus is on quality not quantity. Their artwork and transcripts will be reviewed to assess their skill level and aptitude to succeed. Portfolios are typically presented in person; in the event that doesn't happen, some schools will allow students to mail in slides if distance is an issue. With technology, it's easy and almost expected for students to have electronic portfolios, and possibly with a following. When dealing with art portfolios, there is no simple formula for success due to the level of creativity other than a demonstration of hard work. The key is to be able to demonstrate their talent and show a pattern of their skill, commitment to it, and passion over time. Lastly, it is important to note that there is no such thing as a perfect portfolio, nor any specific style or direction to achieve one.

Tips for Building a Strong Portfolio:

✓ Study various schools for their requirements. Every school has its own set of requirements, and you want to ensure you can demonstrate what's expected.

✓ Create a clean and organized portfolio. Your portfolio should tell a story and not confuse the audience.

✓ Digitize your work in addition to having a physical portfolio.

✓ Ensure your work is protected, but do it without compromising your artistic presence.

✓ Show diversity and depth in your work through technical ability and a variety of genres, techniques, and types.

✓ It should tell a story and communicate who you are, and demonstrate your personality on top of your technical abilities.

✓ Choose quality over quantity. You want to have the right type of pieces versus having a certain number.

✓ It's never too early to start. You should show a progression of your talent over time.

✓ Attend National Portfolio Day. This is your time to show off what you've been doing for the past few years, visit with counselors, and meet the faculty from art and design schools as well as admissions team members before applying to college. Check out nationalportfolioday.org. It's a great way to get feedback and have your portfolio critiqued.

✓ It's okay to include original works and works-in-progress.

✓ Begin and create with the end in mind. Reflect on your vision (future goals) and craft a portfolio that speaks to that and not just admission requirements.

THEATER AUDITIONS

Most liberal arts colleges have a separate admissions process from the auditioning process. In this case, they do not require students to be accepted into the theater department just because they audition (the common exception is if the college offers a Bachelor of Fine Arts (BFA) program). Therefore, it is important that you apply to the college of your choice prior to scheduling an audition. You should also consider spending a full day on campus so that you may talk with theater faculty members and students, attend classes, meet with their admission counselor, and tour the facilities. If possible, do this prior to their audition as a means of building rapport and getting a better feel of the environment.

Although colleges and universities have different requirements, you should prepare two contrasting monologues taken from plays of their choice if you're auditioning for a B.F.A. acting program. Musical theater requirements generally consist of one up-tempo musical selection and one ballad, as well as one monologue from a play or musical of their choice. The total of all pieces should not exceed five minutes. Music for the accompanist, a resume of their theater experience, and a photo are also required.

Tips for a Successful Audition:

✓ Choose material suitable for their age.

✓ If you choose their monologue from a book of monologues, you should read the entire play and be familiar with the context of their selection.

✓ Select a monologue that allows you to speak directly to another person; you should play only one character.

✓ Memorize your selection.

✓ Avoid using characterization or style, as they tend to trap you rather than tapping deeper into inner resources.

As a last note, many schools have required reading lists and writing samples. Contact the targeted schools of choice and view their website or social media pages to identify if this is a requirement and what the list entails. The goal is to be ready and stay ahead of the curve.

Afterwards, the only thing left to do is to apply for college and get those acceptance letters in the mail.

CHAPTER TAKEAWAYS

1. Key Learnings (what you didn't know before):

_____

_____

_____

_____

2. What You Need to Unlearn or Stop Doing:

_____

_____

_____

_____

3. What You Need to Do Next:

_____

_____

_____

_____

CHAPTER 4
FINANCIAL AID & PAYING FOR COLLEGE

Tell me and I'll forget. Show me, and I may not remember. Involve me, and I'll understand.

Native American Proverb

Financial aid is funding available to students in the US attending a post-secondary institution. This funding is provided as grants, loans, scholarships, and work study to assist in covering the high costs of college. The goal of financial aid is to fill in the gap between the cost of college and what a family is expected to pay. It is not intended to cover the entire balance.

Families must complete an application and provide essential information regarding their assets and availability of money. In simple terms, the government will use their formulas to process the data provided and determine how much money your family is eligible for. Based on eligibility, colleges quantify eligibility in the form of a financial award. This is communicated in the financial aid packages sent to high school seniors. Based on a family's application and the eligibility determination, families will either be offered a package comprised of "free" money (scholarships and grants) or loans (money that must be paid back).

Before we dig deeper into the types of financial aid and other ways to fund post-secondary education, let's take a look at some basic terminology so you can properly understand this process.

TERMS AND LANGUAGE

The financial aid process is often confused by many, especially when it comes to the language used in the application and informational packets. Because the process of applying for financial aid is a competition, with hundreds of thousands of students vying for the same pot of money, it is important to have a clear understanding of what you are getting yourself into and the importance of timing. Here are common terms and acronyms you and your family need to know and understand:

COA: Cost of Attendance

EFC: Expected Family Contribution (will be retired in 2022)

FAA: Financial Aid Administrator

FAFSA: Free Application for Federal Student Aid

FWS: Federal Work Study Program

PLUS: Parent Loan for Undergraduate Students

SAP: Satisfactory Academic Progress

SAR: Student Aid Report

SEOG: Supplemental Educational Opportunity Grant

SAI: Student Aid Index (will be used starting 2022 school year, replacing EFC)

NEED

The main purpose of the FAFSA is to determine the student's level of need. This is defined by the Department of Education as the difference between how much college costs (COA) and how much you can actually pay (EFC). So, the formula is: Need = COA - EFC

COST OF ATTENDANCE (COA)

COA is the total cost required to attend college per year. As described in the previous modules, tuition costs vary based on the type of school. Therefore, the COA will be affected also. At most private schools, tuition is the dominant factor in COA, whereas room and board is the overarching number for many public schools.

When estimating COA, you will look at the following areas:

- Tuition
- Room and board
- Fees
- Books
- Living expenses
- Meals
- Transportation

- Personal expenses
- Dependent care
- Computer purchase
- Costs related to a disability or medical condition
- Costs for Eligible Study Abroad Program
- Entertainment

As COA relates to financial aid and determining need, the higher the estimate, the better. A high COA will give the assumption that the need is greater, which makes you eligible for more need-based aid.

EXPECTED FAMILY CONTRIBUTION (EFC)

As stated, EFC is determined by the Department of Education and it is their perception of what they think you can pay toward a college education. Depending on how much you and the family have in assets, savings, investments, and how accurately you complete the FAFSA, the EFC can be any number under $999,999. This number may seem high, but don't worry because there is non-need based aid available.

You may still be wondering how EFC is determined. When you fill out the FAFSA, it requires you to provide personal information such as family size, marital status, and number of dependents, income, and assets. An organization known as the Federal Processor calculates their level of eligibility for financial aid using the "federal methodology."

Please note that many schools, typically Ivy Leagues, require additional information with the FAFSA to determine need and eligibility for non-federal aid, such as completion of a Financial Aid CSS Profile. Also, colleges usually have their own financial aid forms and base their decision on what they call the "institutional methodology." This is often a stricter process that takes into account the value of any property in addition to their assets, which the FAFSA does not do. Therefore, it is important to find out the requirements for the school you are seeking application for. That is why it is also important to contact the school immediately once you have decided upon a college or university. In addition, find out the required deadlines to allow ample time for completion, as these may differ from the federal deadline. The earlier you submit your child's applications, the better. Please note that all schools are not equal when it comes to financial aid because they have different guidelines, distribute monies differently, and fund students differently.

Due to the work of advocates on behalf of low-income families in showing how their expected contributions should be less than $0, the Appropriations Bill renamed EFC to Student Aid Index (SAI) to make it clear that the number a family sees in the SAR isn't the amount of money they're required to pay for college. It will instead be an indicator of what their true financial need is so schools can identify students with the greatest need for assistance.

SAI can be a negative or positive value, showing a range in quantifying the level of need.

NEED-BASED AID

Now that you know what "need" is, let's see how it is defined. Need = COA - EFC, meaning grades, activities, and test scores have no bearings on need-based aid. Also note that this is true until SAI goes into effect.

If it is determined that you qualify for need because the EFC is lower than the COA, you will likely qualify for the following need-based aid:

- Pell Grants - largest source of need-based aid, and is awarded to those with greatest need

- Supplemental Educational Opportunity Grants (SEOG) – also awarded to those with the most financial need, usually Pell Grant recipients

- Academic Competitiveness Awards - visit www.ed.gov and search for ACG State Programs

- National SMART (Science and Mathematics Access to Retain Talent) Grants

- Most college work study

- Most state grants - visit www.ed.gov/erod and click on applicable state/territory

- The Subsidized Portion of the Stafford Loan

- Scholarships and tuition waivers

NON-NEED BASED AID

This is aid that includes awards, scholarships, and tuition waivers based on merit or other factors, including academics, athletics, and musical talents. Federal sources for non-need based aid include Unsubsidized Stafford Loans and the Parent Loans for Undergraduate Students (PLUS). Although these are helpful resources, they are the least desirable because they have stricter repayment policies than Subsidized Stafford Loans.

You may be wondering what the difference is between these loan options.

- The PLUS Loan - a parent loan backed by the federal government and carries a higher interest rate than the other loans. Repayment begins 30 to 45 days after the loan is made and often have a 10 to 15-year repayment period

- Unsubsidized Stafford Loan - guaranteed by the federal government and starts accruing interest while the child is still in school

- The Subsidized Stafford Loan - guaranteed by the federal government and doesn't start accruing interest until six months after the child graduates.

  Be sure to investigate all options prior to signing any paperwork and choose wisely. If you need a loan for the first year, a loan will be needed to pay for all college years. But also understand this: there is no guarantee you will qualify for the same loan and loan amount every year. Be prepared for this potential gap.

FINANCIAL AID FORMS

The greatest challenge of the financial aid process is understanding and mastering the completion of the FAFSA. Although the form may appear intimidating and you may believe that it requires too much personal information, don't let it keep you from applying for aid. Believe or not, the form has gotten easier over the years as technology has evolved and it is slated for yet another overhaul. The Appropriations Bill cuts the number of required questions from 108 to 36 and the number of questions to be completed will be indicative of a family's individual financial situation.

The following information is provided to help you understand the basics. In addition, there are many resources available to assist you with the process. There is the Department of Education student website at www. studentaid.ed.gov, the Federal Student Aid Information Center at 1-800-4-FED-AID (1-800-433-3243), and you can also reach out to your child's guidance or financial aid counselors at school. Do not pay anyone for assistance with completing the form. You can seek the assistance of qualified financial advisors or college planners to help you strategize, re-align assets, and legally work through loopholes that decrease a family's taxable income in an attempt to drastically increase aid award.

STUDENT AID REPORT (SAR)

This is the report you will receive back from the Department of Education after completing and submitting the FAFSA. The SAR will provide you with their EFC. You will want to apply as early as possible in order to receive their EFC in enough time to plan accordingly. Their EFC tells you whether you are eligible for certain kinds of financial aid, along with informing you of their overall level of need. It is highly recommended that you complete and submit their FAFSA electronically because it is free, efficient, and faster than the paper and snail mail process.

THE PROFILE

As stated before, many schools require an additional form known as the College Scholarship Services (CSS)/Financial Aid PROFILE Application. Schools require this supplemental application because they believe the FAFSA is too simple and don't request enough information. The PROFILE takes into account additional assets not provided on the FAFSA such as their parents' home equity amount in their primary residence. Consequently, students qualify for less aid. There will be an opportunity to explain why you qualify for more financial aid, but note that there is a fee to complete the PROFILE.

DEADLINES

Time is of the essence when applying for financial aid. In the beginning of this book, it was stated that the process is a competition. Most of the time when students miss out on financial aid, it is because they waited till the last minute to file, or they failed to submit any corrections in a timely manner.

Each school will have its own deadline for both federal and institutional aid, along with deadlines for scholarships. It is in your best interest to apply at the earliest date possible, even if you must estimate the financial figures. The FAFSA used to be available January 1st of each year, but it was changed a few years back, and it now opens October 1st annually. With the new timeline, the need for families to prepare sooner and have a game plan is that much more crucial. When completing the FAFSA, families will report income and tax information from an earlier tax year in what is called the prior-prior year. See the table below for a summary of key dates defined by the Department of Education FAFSA process.

The School Year Attending College	When to submit FAFSA	Tax & Income Year Evaluated
July 1, 2022–June 30, 2023	October 1, 2021–June 30, 2022	2020
July 1, 2023–June 30, 2024	October 1, 2022–June 30, 2023	2021
July 1, 2024–June 30, 2025	October 1, 2023–June 30, 2024	2022
July 1, 2025–June 30, 2026	October 1, 2024–June 30, 2025	2023
July 1, 2026–June 30, 2027	October 1, 2025–June 30, 2026	2024
July 1, 2027–June 30, 2028	October 1, 2026–June 30, 2027	2025
July 1, 2028–June 30, 2029	October 1, 2027–June 30, 2028	2026

The awarding of financial aid is not only based on eligibility, but the availability of funds as well. Hence, it is highly recommended that families apply early in the process to increase their chance of receiving the aid they qualify for. Funds are oftentimes limited and based on a first come, first served basis.

OTHER FUNDING RESOURCES

Planning ahead can make all the difference when it comes to paying for college. The more time you allow to plan, save, and invest, the more funds you can accumulate. It's like building your retirement plan; you want time to build and let money grow. Paying for college requires at minimum $150,000 to cover five years of attendance. As with any sound investment strategy, having a financial plan that's diverse is the best way to accumulate the desired funds, but to also withstand the variability in investing.

However, the other aspect of getting college funded is to set the expectations for your student by defining their role in this process. What they choose to do or not to do, and how you hold them accountable or not, is directly correlated to how much money you must curate over time to cover the cost of attendance. The most important role your child plays to aid in paying for college is to take rigorous courses and perform well in high school, achieve extra-curricular and community achievement, and deliver higher than average test scores on their PSAT, SAT and/or ACT.

Another contributing factor is their involvement in the scholarship search process. Scholarships are available as early as kindergarten, and it is not a process you wait until junior or senior year to begin. Starting early allows you to start searching and identifying possible scholarships prior to applying for them. Every hour of community service and every tenth of a grade point you earn as a freshman, sophomore, and junior in high school can lead to potential scholarships.

529 PLANS

A 529 plan, one of the most popular options when saving for college, is an education savings plan that allows you the opportunity to pay now for qualified educational expenses in the future. The earlier you start saving money through this plan, the better off you will be. The original intent of the program was to serve as a tax advantaged investment plan designed to encourage families to save for college. 529 plans did for higher education what the 401K did for retirement. The 2017 Tax Cuts and Jobs Act expanded its coverage to include K-12 tuition at private schools. Then in 2019, the SECURE Act expanded the focus further to allow up to $10,000 to be used to pay off the beneficiary's student loans and an additional $10,000 for the student loans of each of the beneficiary's siblings.

Contributions grow tax-deferred, and any money may be withdrawn tax-free if used for qualified education expenses at eligible institutions. In addition, families may be able to take advantage of tax deductions or credits for contributions against their state's taxable income as an additional incentive. Families can learn more details in their state by visiting the College Savings Plans Network (CSPN) website at www.collegesavings.org.

There are two broad types of 529 plans: prepaid tuition plans and education savings plans.

1. Prepaid tuition plans allow you to pre-purchase a defined amount of tuition today, either in years or credits based on today's rates, for attendance at an institution of higher education tomorrow. This allows you to attend college later without having to pay the increased cost of tuition. Details of this plan vary from state to state.

2. Education savings plans allow families to save in a variety of investment vehicles with many options, including equity-based investment options, stable value, guaranteed options, and certificate of deposit-based options. Most 529 plans offer a variety of age-based investment options where the underlying investments become more conservative as the beneficiary gets closer to college age.

As with anything, there are pros and cons to what is being offered. In this case, here are some of the benefits and caveats.

529 Pros:

- Earnings grow tax-deferred
- Distributions are tax-exempt when used for college costs
- Accounts benefit from state-tax exemptions or deductions

- Can be opened for both relatives and friends
- Can choose how money is invested in the savings plan
- Accounts can be transferred to other family members
- Accounts and be refunded, but with penalties
- No income limitations
- IRS gift-tax rules offer an accelerated giving benefit
- Fewer limits for usage than with other college savings plans
- 529 Cons:
- Plan fees may make this a poor choice for short-term planning
- Withdrawing funds results in a 10% penalty
- Funds used for anything outside of school will be taxed
- Prepaid tuition plans may reduce eligibility for other financial aid
- College savings plan accounts in their name will be assessed at 20%
- Prepaid tuition plan funds must be used within a limited time period
- Time extension may come with a penalty
- Funds can't be used for most foreign schools

- Funds can't be used for schools not considered "eligible" institutions of higher education. The definition of "eligible" can vary by state, but schools who file for bankruptcy relief or who violated regulations related to student admittance are common reasons for ineligibility.

Take note that as laws change, the pros and cons will change as well. Always check your local state requirements for current benefits and constraints.

COVERDELL ESAS

The Coverdell Education Savings Account, formerly known as the Education IRA, is another viable option for long-term college savings planning. It is a trust or custodial account set up in the US solely for paying for qualified education expenses for the designated beneficiary of the account.

These accounts are extremely flexible and offer marked advantages over the 529 plans. Just as with the 529, there are drawbacks and benefits. It can also be used for qualified K-12 expenses. Accounts can only be established for children under the age of 18 or with special needs. All requirements must be met when setting an account up, designated as a Coverdell ESA, and in writing.

Coverdell Pros:

- Unlimited investment options

- Few limits are placed on where the funds may be used
- Accounts may be set up at any brokerage firm
- No expiration date for Coverdell tax benefits
- Withdrawals for qualified educational expenses are tax-free
- Coverdell Cons:
- $2,000 annual contribution limit
- Varying setup fees and other administrative costs
- Income limitations on who may participate
- Accounts are counted as a student asset in the needs-analysis formula, which greatly reduces other aid eligibility
- Funds generally must be used before the student reaches 30 years of age

OTHER PLANS

Outside of the 529 and Coverdell ESA plans, you can utilize your own investments and/or map out viable options with a financial planner. In addition, you have the following two options to include in your long-term planning strategy.

- Custodial Accounts - also known as Uniform Gift to Minors Act (UGMA) accounts or Uniform Transfer to Minors Act (UTMA) accounts. These plans allow parents to save money and invest, and maintain full control until their child is an adult. Both accounts allow parents to transfer financial assets to a minor without establishing a trust.

There are tax advantages for this plan, along with a benefit rate at which the account earnings are taxed. A person can contribute up to $15,000 annually without incurring a gift tax ($30,000 per married couple). The first $1,100 of a child's unearned income is tax-free. The next $1,100 is taxed at the child's lower federal rate, and anything beyond that is taxed at the custodian's federal rate. Between the age of 18 to 25, contingent upon the state requirements, all funds in the account must become property of the beneficiary, who can legally spend the money on anything, not just college. A major caveat is that money from these accounts, and others like them, are viewed as an asset for the child. When it comes to the FAFSA, dependent assets are assessed at a higher value that reduces aid eligibility by 20% of the asset value. In comparison, when 529s are in the parent's name (and therefore viewed as a parental asset), aid is reduced by up to 5.46% of the asset value.

- Savings bonds are backed by the full faith and credit of the US government and are considered one of the safest investments. They offer as many of the same benefits, including tax exemption when used to cover the costs of education.

- If you find yourself not in a position to start early and you are late in the game, there are potential options for you to review and pursue.

- Tax strategies - examines how you fill out your tax forms. By focusing on minimizing adjusted growth income you report during the year financial aid is determined (see the FAFSA table and dates previously shared), families can reap the benefits of better aid packages.

- Education tax credits help with the cost of higher education by reducing the amount of taxes owed each year. The type of tax credits available will vary as tax laws change. Currently, the two education credits available are the American Opportunity Tax Credit and the Lifetime Learning Credit. Be sure to visit www.irs.gov for the latest details and recent changes.

- Student income protection is the amount of income a student or parent can make in a year before that income is counted against them for financial aid. This allows an individual or a family to exclude a certain amount of income before it becomes a factor in the FAFSA financial aid equation. Note that the dollar amount will vary depending on the size of the family. Student income is assessed with stricter rules because of the lack of need for them to use their earnings to pay for household needs, such as food and shelter. Therefore, parents should never put assets in their name. Dependent student income is protected up to $6,970 and independent students have an income allowance of $10,840. Anything a dependent earns above this amount will impact the amount of financial aid they qualify for depending on family size and the number of students in college.

Exceptions to this rule are either jobs or spending opportunities that are considered exempt such as:

- Work-study income
- Money from cooperative learning opportunities provided through the college
- AmeriCorps educational awards provided under the National and Community Service Act of 1990

Please note the terms of these plans, as amounts and strategies can change as legislature and laws are modified. For example, recent changes were due to an increase in the Consumer Price Index (CPI) and price inflation. Always obtain the latest information by reviewing the Department of Education and state websites or consult a tax accountant or financial advisor for accurate details.

DECLARING DEPENDENCY

Your child may say they are providing for themselves and funding their lifestyle and path to college. Therefore, you feel your income status is not applicable to their financial aid application, which means that they can receive more money. The Department of Education will not declare your child as independent and will no longer include your income and assets when calculating financial aid unless you can answer "yes" to any of the following questions:

1. Will you be 24 or older by January 1 of the school year for which you are applying financial aid?

2. At the beginning of the current school year, will you be working on a master's or doctorate degree?

3. As of today, are you married or separated but not divorced?

4. Are you responsible for a child who receives 51% or more of their support from you?

5. Are you the caretaker or have responsibility for a dependent (excluding children and a spouse) that lives with you and or receive 51% or more of their support from you now or until the end of the school year?

6. At any time since you turned age 13, were both of your parents deceased, were you in foster care, or were you a ward or dependent of the court?

7. Are you currently serving on an active duty in the US Armed Forces for purposes other than training?

8. Are you a veteran of the US Armed Forces?

9. Have you been granted a legal guardianship or given the status as an emancipated minor by a court?

10. Do you fall in one or more of the following categories: homeless, at risk of being homeless, or an unaccompanied youth?

As you can see, there are fewer options when you compare long-term planning with short-term planning strategies. The key is to be prepared and strategic in your approach when it comes to funding.

WHERE IS THE "FREE" MONEY?

Positioning your child to receive what is classified as "free" money in the forms of grants and scholarships requires preparation and knowledge of what is out there and where to find it. Their ultimate goal and desire is to get someone else to fund their college education. That means you not only want to rely on aid from the school and government, but you will also want to search for scholarships provided by corporations, and private and public organizations. This "free" money can come in many forms such as federal grants, state grants, private scholarships, institutional scholarships, federal scholarships, service awards, fellowships, tuition waivers, housing allowances, and forgivable loans. You must be ready to identify the right people, organizations, and groups, and start networking.

SCHOLARSHIPS

Scholarships can be won for any number of accomplishments, including academics, athletics, music, and even hobbies, interests, or initiatives. There is literally (almost) a scholarship for everything and anything, and it's not just about academics and money. But scholarships are either categorized as a general funding source or they have specific qualification categories such as ethnicity, degree majors, gender, organization affiliation, disability, etc. There are varying types of scholarships ranging from private, institutional, and federal to merit and need-based.

Private scholarships can come from anyone and anywhere for any number of reasons. You generally must pursue these scholarships on your own, independent of the college you apply to. Keep in mind that colleges can count private scholarships as aid when determining your financial aid award. For this reason, it is wise to compare multiple colleges and investigate how they classify private scholarships when determining your overall level of need for financial aid. It's essential for you to know if they will decrease the amount of financial aid you are eligible for or if it will be excluded from the overall formula.

Institutional scholarships come directly from the college endowments or foundations, which the financial aid offices can count as aid when determining need for financial aid packages. It is important to note that some are part of the packaging process, while others require a separate application process and deadline. Therefore, you should always search the school's website for details, ask the financial aid officer for direction, and get an understanding about how this award and external awards will affect funds awarded in your financial aid package.

Federal scholarships are federally funded scholarship programs. An example is the Truman Scholarship (www.

truman.gov), supporting future generations who answer the call to public service leadership for the past forty years. Because most of these scholarships are not highly publicized, it is recommended that you become familiar with the Department of Education website (www.ed.gov), social media platforms, and also search for scholarships on the internet. In addition, you can find valuable scholarship and application information on free scholarship search engines. There are so many resources, and here a few of the more popular pages:

1. fastweb.com
2. scholarshipamerica.org
3. collegenet.com
4. niche.com
5. cappex.com
6. collegboard.com
7. scholarships.com

Scholarship contests offer you a chance to roll the dice and compete for a chance to win scholarship dollars. Before applying for these, be warned and skeptical of any contest that has any fees involved. Here is a sample list of legitimate and free scholarship contests:

1. National Peace Essay Contest (usip.org)
2. Society for Professional Journalists (spj.org/a-hs.asp)
3. Coca-Cola Scholars Foundation Contest (coca-colascholars.org)

4. Abraham Lincoln Contest (thelincolnforum.org)

5. Ayn Rand (aynrand.org)

6. Duck Tape Club (ducktapeclub.com)

Memorial assistance takes the form of scholarships offered to assist those affected by national tragedies or relatives of police officers, firefighters, or soldiers who lost their lives in the line of duty. You should search at a federal and state level for these offerings, as you may fall under multiple categories.

As a note of caution, be aware of scholarship scams. Most scams ask for payments up front and offer guarantees that you will receive money for college. Any legitimate source will never require you to pay a fee, and there are no guarantees when it comes to scholarship awards. But know there are a few credible exceptions. One that's popular with a fee tied to it for operating fees is the Scholly App. It doesn't guarantee any winnings; it only provides a platform to apply to legitimate scholarships. Read the fine print and exercise caution. Because there is great need and many families are confused about the process, scammers use these families' vulnerabilities and emotions to rack up money without delivering results.

SERVICE AWARDS

Service awards are given to individuals who dedicate their time, life, and efforts to others. Not only is there a financial reward in doing so, it looks great on a resume when applying for jobs.

Below, a look at the types of service awards you can apply for:

AmeriCorps offers up to $10,000 in scholarships for those who perform community service. If AmeriCorps money is used to repay student loans, you do not have to report it to the financial aid office. Therefore, it will not decrease financial aid dollars. Visit www.americorps.org for details.

Armed Forces can be very rewarding when it comes to paying for college education. Each branch has various offerings and award levels, so investigate, ask questions, and assess if there is a proper fit. You want to consider the branch that's better suited for your long-term career goals, length of service versus benefits, college restrictions, and other requirements. When I traveled the US for our college expos, I got to learn more about the branches and their offerings. My overall conclusion was that people are misinformed and should be better educated on how this viable option can actualize their college dreams without debt (and war, for that matter). Look beyond the money and dissect the levels and accompanying options. You have the ROTC, Reserves, Active Duty and Military Academies to assess fit for. Do your due diligence and don't discount it as an option until you investigate, because you may be surprised. If your parent is a veteran with educational benefits, have them connect with either or both the school of choice financial aid officer who specializes in veteran's administration (VA) benefits and the VA benefits department to understand what's available. Like everything else, using VA benefits to fund education is not necessarily a straightforward approach. Don't wait until the last minute, because the process takes time.

For those unfamiliar with military academies, they are competitive to gain admittance to.. Students are offered free tuition and graduate as military officers. As stated previously, there is an obligation to the student for these valuable benefits. Get informed and weigh the costs. Here are the four service academies for you to explore if interested:

- The U.S. Military Academy (West Point, New York)

- The U.S. Naval Academy (Annapolis, Maryland)

- The U.S. Air Force Academy (Colorado Springs, Colorado)

- The U.S. Coast Guard Academy (New London, Connecticut)

Fellowships are free money that come in the form of a stipend awarded for a specific purpose, skill, need, or project. Fellowships are generally associated with graduate studies, but there may be some available for undergraduates. This type of aid will not be found in traditional scholarship books and websites because they are typically funded by community-based and nonprofit groups who merge their philanthropic giving with educational opportunities. Therefore, you will have to be savvier with the search process.

MAKING THE BEST DECISION

Money is usually the driving factor in most decisions, especially when it comes to a high-ticket investment like a college education. You want to make sure that the school offering you the aid also provides the total academic package you need. It is not advantageous for you to select a school because they gave you the most money, but they lack the academic program or classes you desire to pursue. Alternatively, the school can have the prestige you want, but they are offering you a small financial aid package, leaving you with an enormous amount of post-college debt. The choice is yours, so choose wisely. Here are a few things to consider:

- There are no guarantees of funds awarded during year one.

- If you need a loan for year one, you will need a loan for the remaining years.

- Freshman year is usually the year that the most aid is needed.

- Assess the number of recurring scholarships vs. one-year scholarships.

The message here is to weigh all options, be in a position to have multiple choices, and make an informed decision that will support your short and long-term plans and goals. As well, don't be afraid to seek qualified advice from a highly respected mentor, counselor, or friend.

Once the decision is made, you will need to sign and submit the acceptance letter by the deadline. You can accept the total offer, or you can decide to only accept part of the package. For example, the school may offer grants, scholarships, and loans and you may decide to only take the grants and scholarships. Whatever you decide, make sure you have the full picture of their total COA to ascertain if you will have a gap. If you do choose to accept a loan, borrow wisely by only taking out what you need. Do not look at this as an opportunity to spend frivolously on unnecessary items such as clothes, cars, trips, gadgets, and so forth. Look at the statistics: paying back student loans is a beast and can limit how life is lived post-college.

In the event you decline the option to take out a loan, know that you can always reapply if you later find out it is needed to cover your child's expenses.

CHAPTER TAKEAWAYS

1. Key Learnings (what you didn't know before):

_____

_____

_____

_____

2. What You Need to Unlearn or Stop Doing:

_____

_____

_____

_____

3. What You Need to Do Next:

_____

_____

_____

_____

CHAPTER 5
COLLEGE ENTRANCE EXAMS

Today's preparation determines tomorrow's achievement.

Unknown Source

Hearing the word "test" may send your child and even you into a nervous tailspin, especially after what everyone experienced during the COVID pandemic. Unfortunately, it is still a reality of life and one of the main components for either getting accepted into a major post-secondary institution and receiving financial aid. The SAT and ACT are used by colleges to determine the level of readiness of a student and their ability to successfully complete a college curriculum. Schools are essentially assessing the risk level of a student. Therefore, it is not something to take lightly or procrastinate in preparing for.

Prior to taking either one of these tests, students can prepare by taking the PSAT (a preliminary version of the SAT), the actual SAT, and/or the ACT Aspire. All three tests use an evidentiary approach to measure a student's current academic development level of achievement in math, reading, writing, English, and science (note that only ACT includes the science segment). Used properly, parents, students, and school counselors can develop targeted learning plans that set a student on a path of high performance academically and on the actual SAT and ACT.

Let's look at each test individually. Before we do that, note that the best way to maximize the benefits of taking these tests is to prepare for them. Even if your child is an honor student, they still need to study and understand the intricacies of the test, the science behind the structure of it, and the test strategies needed to master it. Preparing for the test is an ongoing process that you should start preparing for at the elementary school level. Here are a few ways to set your child up for success:

- Take challenging courses at school
- Complete homework, aiming for the highest grade possible
- Prepare for tests and quizzes and perform well on them
- Ask and answer practice questions for both the pre-tests and actual tests
- Work with a tutor
- Take a test prep class for both the pre-tests and actual tests

We may not like tests, but until the process changes, learn how to maximize this requirement and win with it. Schools at all levels use these types of tests to determine who qualifies for gifted programs, academic competitions and opportunities, dual credit, and other advantageous benefits.

Let's look at the types of tests involved in the college readiness life cycle, starting with pre-tests that families can use to prepare for the ACT or SAT.

PSAT

The Preliminary SAT qualifying test is a program co-sponsored by The College Board and National Merit Scholarship Corporation (NMSC) and is offered in October. It is a standardized test that provides firsthand practice for the SAT, along with the opportunity to enter NMSC (www.nationalmerit.org) scholarship programs and gain access to college and career planning tools based off the junior year score.

The PSAT measures critical reading, math problem-solving, and writing skills. It is a measurement of skills acquired both in and out of school, and not surrounding specific facts from their classes. There are several benefits to taking the PSAT:

- Receive feedback on strengths and weaknesses regarding skills necessary for college study
- Learn how performance on an admissions test might compare with that of others who apply to college
- Enter the competition for scholarships from NMSC during their junior year of high school
- Help prepare for the SAT
- Receive information from colleges when you check "yes" to Student Search Service

Most students take the PSAT for the first time during their sophomore year, but the earlier a student is exposed, the greater chance they will be more prepared and comfortable with the test dynamics. It's all about exposure.

Gaining insight early on will give them a preliminary feel of what to expect, so they'll know the areas to focus more on prior to taking it during their junior year when it is used to determine National Merit Scholars.

There is also the PSAT 10. The PSAT/NMSQT and PSAT 10 are basically the same test, but offered at different times of the year. Here are some common benefits outlined by The College Board:

- They are both great practice for the SAT because they test the same skills and knowledge as the SAT, in a way that makes sense for your grade level.

- They both provide score reports you can use to personalize your Khan Academy® SAT practice.

- The score reports also list which AP courses you should check out.

You should speak to your child's counselor on identifying the best test to take, but note that you can advocate to have your child take it sooner. At minimum, have them take it in 10th grade as a dry run and preparation for the 11th grade. Visit The College Board for the latest and greatest details, as things are always changing and this is a fluid process.

PSAT/NMSQT vs. PSAT 10		
Facts and Features	PSAT/NMSQT	PSAT 10
Who takes the test?	10th- and 11th-graders	10th-graders
Where do students take it?	At school	At school
When do students take it?	Fall (view PSAT/NMSQT calendar)	Spring (view PSAT 10 calendar)
Does the National Merit®Scholarship Program use scores to find eligible students?	Yes	No
Does the test connect students to other scholarships?	Yes	Yes

Scores are officially reported by The College Board via schools, districts, and states. Students can access their scores earlier using their online account. When it comes to NMSC, they receive the scores as the test's co-sponsor, along with the following scholarship and recognition programs:

- National Hispanic Recognition Program
- National Scholarship Service
- Telluride Seminar Scholarships

Note that colleges do not have access to these scores, but students can opt-in to Student Search Service, a free program that helps students connect to colleges and nonprofit scholarship agencies. Opting in will not release your scores, but other limited personal information will be shared so that the connection can be made. These are a few of the scholarship partners in this category:

- United Negro College Fund (UNCF)
- Hispanic Scholarship Fund
- Jack Kent Cooke Foundation
- Asian & Pacific Islander American Scholarship Fund
- American Indian Graduate Center

Again, things change often so check for latest information. Learn more about the test, scores, dates, rankings, and more at www.collegeboard.com/student/testing/psat/about.html.

ACT ASPIRE

ACT Aspire is a longitudinal assessment used to connect student performance with readiness benchmarks in English, math, reading, science, and writing for grades 3 through 10. It is a modular test, which means many students will NOT take all four subject tests. This precludes students from having a composite score, like with the ACT, until they reach the 8th grade. Students between grades 8 and 10 will get a composite score similar to that of ACT in the four primary areas, scaled from 400 to 499. But when it comes to younger ACT Aspire students, their scoring model can be converted to the ACT's 0 to 36 scales, using ACT's conversion table. This can then serve as a preparation and predictive tool that identifies strengths and areas where the greatest improvement is needed.

At the present time, ACT Aspire is not a tool for public consumption. It is primarily available to schools, enabling them to enroll entire classrooms and gauge the level of learning per grade level. Unlike the PSAT, ACT Aspire is not deemed equivalent to National Merit. As things change and continue to evolve, anything can happen in the near future. Stay informed and prepared.

ACT Aspire has replaced the PLAN, which was a practice for the ACT and whose report also identified career interest areas.

Again, these tests are part of the college readiness lifecycle, but they are very different from the actual college entrance exams. You will use the pre-test discussed previously as a precursor to taking the real college entrance exams and as a tool for mapping out a study plan that yields results on the actual exams.

When it comes to applying for college, you will use one or both of the official college entrance exams, ACT and SAT. Yes, there's talk about the need for these exams, the value they add, and the inequities that exist. I am not here to debate any of that, but I am here to give you the main points so that you understand the process. Let's learn more about each test below.

SAT

The SAT is the other assessment tool used in the application process by colleges and universities in the U S. Its approach to predicting college success is different from the ACT in that it measures critical thinking and problem solving capabilities. Governed by The College Board and administered by a national testing organization, Educational Testing Service (ETS), which facilitates the testing process across the country. Prior to COVID, the test was only given seven times a year, but the pandemic has increased the frequency of exam offerings.

Until things settle after the pandemic, here's the basic construct for the SAT. The SAT is a multiple-choice, pencil-and paper test that the student is allotted three hours to complete. A student's aptitude is measured by their performance in the following sections:

- Math - 80 minutes; 58 questions focused on algebra, problem solving, data analysis, advanced math, and topics like geometry, trigonometry, and pre-calculus
- Evidence-Based Reading - 65 minutes; 52 questions covering reading and vocabulary in context
- Evidence-Based Writing - 35 minutes; 44 questions assessing grammar and its usage.

Each section is scored from 200 to 800 (Math & Evidence-Based Reading & Writing), yielding a total range of 400 to 1600 points.

There used to be SAT Subject Tests, which measured a student's knowledge and skills in particular subject areas and their ability to apply that knowledge, used as an additional measurement of academic achievement. At the peak of the COVID pandemic, The College Board made the decision to discontinue both the subject tests and optional essay. With this being a fluid process, the uncertainties around testing, and the varying requirements, some schools are supplementing missing tests or subject tests with AP or IB Tests.

As always, verify requirements with the schools of interest, understanding that each school could have a different requirement. Unfortunately, it's not a "one-size fits all" model. You also want to monitor test requirement changes on The College Board's website at https://collegereadiness. collegeboard.org/sat.

ACT

The ACT is also a college entrance exam that predicts a student's ability to succeed in college. It is a measurement of a students' knowledge level via a multiple-choice test assessing four areas: English, mathematics, reading and science. You can see the immediate differences from the SAT, including the Optional Writing Test that gauges a student's ability to plan and write a short essay. Please note that with The College Board discontinuing the SAT Writing Test during the pandemic, as well as the pressure surrounding access to college entrance exams, I wouldn't be surprised if the ACT Optional Writing Test will be on the chopping block next. Check the website or their social media pages for the latest updates.

At any rate, let's learn the basics concerning the ACT. Like the SAT, the ACT is an entrance exam used by most colleges and universities to make admissions and funding decisions. It too is a multiple-choice, pencil-and-paper test administered by ACT, Inc., and is used to measure a student's readiness for college.

In examining how the ACT differs from the SAT, the differences lie in the structure, subject areas, and approach. The test lasts two hours and fifty-five minutes (excluding the Writing Test) and three hours and thirty-five minutes (including the Writing Test). The test is broken down into the following areas:

- English: 45 minutes; 75 questions measuring the level of understanding of English (grammar, punctuation, sentence structure, and rhetorical skills), production of writing, and knowledge of language skills.

- Mathematics: 60 minutes; 60 questions measuring mathematical skills acquired in courses like algebra I and II, geometry, and some trigonometry.

- Reading: 35 minutes; 40 questions measuring reading comprehension commonly encountered in prose fiction, social studies, natural sciences, and humanities.

- Science: 35 minutes; 40 questions measuring the interpretation, analysis, evaluation, reasoning, and problem-solving skills required in biology, chemistry, Earth/space sciences, and physics. Questions can include graphs, charts, tables, and research summaries.

- Writing (optional): 40 minutes; measures writing skills taught in English and entry-level college composition courses.

Each section is scored on a scale of 1 to 36, yielding a composite score between 1 to 36, as the average of the four sections.

In addition to this, just as the SAT connects you to scholarships, ACT established a partnership with STEM Premier in 2014 to enhance opportunities for all students, especially those who are underserved in the area of STEM (science, technology, engineering, and math). Through STEM Premier, students can qualify for scholarships funded through this partnership and build a profile to draw interest and recognition from colleges and businesses across the country (www.act.org).

WHICH TEST SHOULD YOUR CHILD TAKE?

Almost all competitive schools accept both ACT and SAT scores. Therefore, your child's decision should be based on the school's requirements primarily, and then on the subjects they are stronger in. If all the schools they apply to accept both tests, they should then only take one test multiple times.

So, how do you choose? The SAT is two-thirds critical reading and writing and one-third math. The ACT is one-half English and reading, and one-half math and science. One way of deciding is by subject matter. If you are stronger in English, you might want to take the SAT. If you are a math whiz and science geek, and not so good in English, you might do better on the ACT. The ACT is also a better option for STEM students. The key is to take the test that plays to your child's strengths and give you the biggest advantage, then taking it multiple times alongside a solid test-prep class and testing plan.

Once a test is selected, your child should plan to take the test early in their high school years. I recommend taking it toward the end of their freshman year at the latest to establish a baseline and get an idea of where they are at. Then, build a study plan from there that is focused on scoring high and improving the areas they are weak in. All college entrance exam tests should be completed and the desired score attained no later than the end of their junior year. They should only take the tests during the fall of their senior year if they need to pull their score up a few points for a school or scholarship.

WHAT IS AN ACCEPTABLE SCORE?

The national average for the SAT was around 1500 on the old format, and between 20 and 21 for the ACT; the new SAT average is yet to be determined. But if your child's scores are close to these averages, they will likely be accepted into a post-secondary institution as long as their grades are decent. It may not be their dream school or target school, but some schools will accept them. Remember the more selective schools will have stricter requirements, and so average test scores may not be good enough. Scoring above the benchmarks will improve their chances of getting into a more selective school, along with setting them up to receive merit-based scholarships. Keep in mind that the higher the score, the more opportunities they can attract.

Scores below the average scores are considered low for any major university. This can possibly be overcome with strong grades, a strong essay, or an outstanding application. Even still, if accepted, the school may require students to take remedial courses as a freshman, participate in a bridge program, or attend a community college to prove themselves.

When taking the desired test or tests, students can choose to send either score reports from a single test event, a Superscore for ACT Scores, or from all test events or Score Choice for SAT Scores.

As you can see, the rules for test scores are different for ACT and SAT. SAT has what's called Score Choice, which allows you to send your best scores. Basically, you choose by test date what you want to send to colleges. If you decide not to use Score Choice, all of your scores will be sent to your recipients. You should still feel comfortable sending all scores, since most colleges consider a student's best score. But keep in mind that some colleges and scholarship programs require you to send all your scores. If you choose not to use Score Choice, all your scores will be sent to the colleges you choose.

As with the ACT, you can send four free score reports to colleges and scholarship programs every time you register for the SAT. This is the fastest and most cost-effective way if you don't qualify for an SAT fee waiver. Otherwise, you can send reports after your official scores are released for a per report fee.

ACT will automatically send scores from the single event test date designated on the request and will automatically calculate the ACT Superscore for tests taken after September 2016.

Unless your child gets a perfect score on either test, there is always room for improvement. The key is to start the preparation process early, have them study hard, and practice. Remember that high test scores can help attract additional scholarship money. Invest in a test prep class and learn the various test taking strategies. This pays off royally.

Taking all of this into consideration, if your child takes both tests, there are conversion charts to help you gauge which test score is better. Here's the ACT Composite to SAT Total according to ACT.org:

ACT	SAT	SAT Range
36	1590	1570-1600
35	1540	1530-1560
34	1500	1490-1520
33	1460	1450-1480
32	1430	1420-1440
31	1400	1390-1410
30	1370	1360-1380
29	1340	1330-1350
28	1310	1300-1320
27	1280	1260-1290
26	1240	1230-1250
25	1210	1200-1220
24	1180	1160-1190
23	1140	1130-1150
22	1110	1100-1120
21	1080	1060-1090
20	1040	1030-1050
19	1010	990-1020
18	970	960-980
17	930	920-950
16	890	880-910
15	850	830-870
14	800	780-820
13	760	730-770
12	710	690-720
11	670	650-680
10	630	620-640
9	590	590-610

When we say that these college entrance exams measure college readiness, this is dictated by where a student ranks in terms of each test's benchmarks.

The ACT College Readiness Benchmarks are the minimum ACT test scores required for a student to have a reasonable chance of success in a college credit earning course. Scoring below these benchmarks can result in a denied admissions and lead to a student being placed in remedial courses. There are benchmarks for six ACT test scores taken into consideration. Each is tied to potential performance in a course or set of college courses within the same subject area.

1. English - English Composition I: 18

2. Mathematics - College Algebra: 22

3. Reading - American History, Other History, Psychology, Sociology, Political Science, and Economics: 22

4. Science - Biology: 23

5. STEM - Calculus, Chemistry, Biology, Physics, Engineering: 26

6. ELA - English Composition I, American History, Other History, Psychology, Sociology, Political Science, Economics: 20

Since both the ACT and SAT have benchmarks to measure a student's college readiness risk level, here's how the SAT defines their benchmarks.

1. Evidence-Based Reading and Writing: 480

2. Math: 530

Many students are entering college unprepared for the rigorous demands that college requires, and that is why college entrance exams, along with AP/IB tests, are used to assess a student's risk level in their ability to complete a college matriculation.

HOW DO I PREPARE FOR THE TESTS?

Your child can prepare for both tests first by mapping out and enrolling in the college ready course work as early as middle school, covering the required subjects assessed on the tests. Then they must perform well in these courses by studying and working hard. Building a strong foundation for getting off to the right start really begins earlier than high school. Around the 6th grade, expanded reading, vocabulary exercises, and the like are highly beneficial.

Next, your child can take advantage of supplemental assistance through outside resources. Some of these resources cost hundreds of dollars, while others are free or charge a nominal fee. Proven resource options include:

- Practice Tests: there are plenty of online sites and books with free practice tests available to help your child prepare for the actual test. Some programs and resources include Khan Academy; March2Success. com; The ACT or SAT websites, etc.

- Test Prep Classes: if your child doesn't do well with standardized tests, this option is highly suggested. The classes involve homework and practice tests. Classes are available via online platforms or in a physical classroom, administered by reputable persons or organizations in your local area. You don't have to go with the bigger names, as there are smaller organizations helping students reach higher limits. Regarding the cost, the price tag is usually in the hundreds or more, but it is well worth it when you remember that the cost of college is at least $30,000 per year.

- Individual Tutoring: if your child requires personalized attention to prepare for the ACT or SAT, this option is best. Having face-to-face interactions can help motivate your child to invest the time needed to properly prepare for the tests. Tutors can also tailor their preparation around their strengths and weaknesses, while providing instant feedback and explanations.

Here are some test-taking "to do's" to share with your child that will foster an environment and discipline for learning:

- Study, Study, STUDY! Create a study plan, buy some books or take a class (ideally all of these things).

- Register for the test by the deadline.

- Visit the test center before their test to avoid getting lost, familiarize themselves with the testing environment, etc.

- Take a full-length, timed practice test about three days before the test. Remember, tests must be approached strategically and confidently in order to do well.

- Do NOT leave studying until the day before the test!

- The day before the test, gather a "test day kit" that contains (this can change, so always check the testing site):

  o Calculator with fresh batteries

  o Watch

  o Some number 2 pencils with slightly dull points

  o Erasers

  o Photo ID (passport, driver's license, or student ID)

  o Do relaxation and visualization techniques

  o Get a good night's rest

- Follow these rules on the morning of the test:

  o Eat a substantial breakfast

  o Don't drink a lot of coffee or liquids

  o Dress in layers so it is easier to adjust to the temperature in the testing room

  o Read something like a newspaper or magazine to warm up their brain

  o Arrive early, allowing time for traffic delays or accidents

Another way that not only prepares you for the tests but for college in general is by taking "college ready" courses classified as honors, Advanced Placement (AP) or International Baccalaureate (IB). These courses fall under what is considered rigorous coursework that aligns with college level classes. Consequently, when there have been missing ACT/SAT test scores, colleges have requested AP or IB tests as a tool for assessing readiness. Therefore, having these classes should be part of your child's coursework for a variety of reasons. Let's examine the highlights.

Many high schools offer one of the advanced course pathways in their curriculum. The value of such programs is their ability to offer college-level coursework to high school students as a measurement of their propensity to succeed in college. Course offerings will vary by program to include classes from Computer Science, Spanish, Arts, Statistics to World Languages and Cultures. Students usually have to qualify to take these courses, but you can advocate for your child to be included. There are many benefits, one being the earning of college credit and testing out introductory courses once they get to college. This only happens when a student successfully passes with an acceptable score on the AP and IB exams. Acceptance and scoring will vary from school to school. Be sure to investigate and do your research, then map out a plan of attack.

AP PROGRAM AND EXAMS

Managed by The College Board, Advanced Placement programs are more widespread in schools across the US. AP courses are college-level equivalent courses that get students ready for post-secondary academic performance. These courses represent the rigor needed in seven subject areas and thirty-eight courses to facilitate college-level academics during the high school matriculation. Like many aspects of the college prep process, course availability will vary by school. These are the seven main subject areas students can find courses to pursue under the AP Program: Arts, Math and Computer Sciences, English, History and Social Sciences, World Languages and Cultures, Sciences, and AP Capstone (a two-year program consisting of two courses: AP Seminar and AP Research. Students who successfully complete the program and earn scores of 3 or higher on at least four other AP exams will receive an AP Capstone Diploma or an AP Seminar and Research Certificate.).

Here, some details of the AP course exams:

- Students complete their exams in May

- Exams are two to three hours long

- Wrong answers and unanswered questions are not punitive

- The test has two parts:

  ○ Part one is multiple-choice

  ○ Part two is comprised of free-response questions that can be answered in either an essay, a verbal (conversational), or a problem-solution format.

- Exams are scored based on a five-point scale. A score of five, the highest possible score, means 'extremely qualified'. One, the lowest score indicates 'no recommendation'.

IB PROGRAM AND EXAMS

International Baccalaureate (IB) is an interdisciplinary program focused on college readiness, but with an international mindset. Students are challenged to broaden their educational experience and apply their knowledge and skills in their academics. Like AP Exams, IB Exams could translate into college credits if the student scores high enough. The acceptance of scores will vary by school.

The IB Program focuses on six subject areas identified as either Higher Level (HL) or Standard Level (SL) and students have the option to pursue the Diploma Programme track. The six areas students can choose from are Arts, Language Acquisition, Mathematics, Sciences, Individual and Societies, and Studies in Language and Literature. Characteristics of the exam:

- Enrollment in an IB Class is required to sit for an exam

- Exams can be taken at the completion of a SL or HL class

- Students are assessed based on their ability to think critically and relay global issues

- Students will have to complete assessment tasks at school

- Tasks are internally and/or externally assessed and can be comprised of one or more tasks:
  - External markings: examinations, extended essays, written assignments or tasks, and theory of knowledge essays
  - Internal and external markings: projects, artistic performances, oral work in languages, investigations in mathematics, portfolios, explorations in sciences, and fieldwork in geography
  - Assessment of tasks may be: multiple-choice, performances, essays, short-response questions, presentations, and extended-response questions
- Every test is scored based on a one to seven grading scale. Seven is the highest score and a five or higher is usually what colleges will accept for college credit.

Again, offerings of these advanced courses that represent the rigor colleges are looking for are not always offered at every school. Don't fret, because you can enroll your child in online AP courses through a virtual school and program. So don't let this limit your child's opportunity to strengthen their transcript.

Another great option is enrolling your child in dual enrollment classes at the local community college. Talk to your child's counselor to learn about your state's dual enrollment program and assess which courses are a good fit. This is a great way to let students experience what college is like, and it can help them earn college credit without paying for pricey AP or IB exams.

CHAPTER TAKEAWAYS

1. Key Learnings (what you didn't know before):

_____

_____

_____

_____

2. What You Need to Unlearn or Stop Doing:

_____

_____

_____

_____

3. What You Need to Do Next:

_____

_____

_____

_____

CHAPTER 6
BRAND MANAGEMENT

Technology is like a two-edged sword that cuts coming and going. It can be both a blessing and a curse depending on how it's used. Choose wisely.

Tameka Williamson

In an age of convenience marked by technological advancements, people tend to get more and more relaxed in their ability to think, analyze situations, and problem solve. Compared to a couple decades ago, our culture has evolved from manual processing, cassette and VHS Tapes, and physical workout classes to touch screen or audibly controlled devices, groceries delivered to your front door, smart appliances, and digital workouts using artificial intelligence. Alongside that, social media has evolved into platforms that have created "influencers" who focus on creating content that goes viral and generates millions of views. Who would have imagined this would be how we now communicate and market products, services, and brands to one another?

When you reflect on it, you can see the convenience and accessibility factor, making it easier to expand your network and connect with people globally. But there is a dark side to all of this that can send a college bound or college student's world into a downward spiral. Depending on how these social platforms are used, students can live to regret their level of engagements. Oftentimes, young people don't consider the consequences of their perceived "harmless" act and the long-term effects on their life, their family and others involved. That said, let's explore a few examples on how a "harmless" act can impede their future. To make this easier to follow, I will break them down into the three brackets: social media, texting/email, and phone applications. How your child engages in these three areas can either elevate or minimize their risk level in the eyes of a college or university and scholarship organization.

Social Media

From TikTok, Snapchat, Instagram, and so on, these platforms present many attractive features to the younger generation. They not only become a vehicle for communicating and connecting to people across the globe; it is a great way for them to share ideas and gain notoriety in pursuit of a viral response that can make them the next influencer. I get it; becoming an influencer seems to carry much glitz and glam. Not only that, it can yield a pretty nice paycheck. But there are risks associated with this if a responsible adult doesn't manage or monitor the situation.

Before we get into what's at stake, I'll set the stage by sharing some key platform statistics.

The top three social media platforms among teens as per Statista in 2021 are:

1. Snapchat, with 249 million daily active users

2. TikTok, with more than one billion users (40% of whom are between the ages of 16 and 24). In 2020, downloads of TikTok surpassed those of Facebook, Instagram, and Snapchat

3. Instagram/Instagram Reels, with 2.54 billion daily active visitors

In addition to these popular platforms, keep an eye on Clubhouse, Twitch, and Houseparty which the younger generation uses to communicate. Along with youth, corporations use the same platforms to advertise and market to targeted demographics, expand their footprint, engage in social outreach projects, and a host of other things. These platforms are also used as means of networking, job hunting, reconnecting with friends and family, and staying current on major events, and all of these aspects are great.

The alternative side is where people use it as a means to brag, gossip, bully, and embarrass others, or complain about their school, job, and life in general. Of course, these particular uses, along with the posting of inappropriate pictures, are the activities that can get your child into trouble. Just like the phrase, "What happens in Vegas, stays in Vegas;" we can also say, "What happens on social media, stays on social media." Once it's posted, regardless of the platform, it creates a digital footprint that cannot be erased. Yes, this also includes disappearing SnapChats and deleted posts.

As a result, the improper messages can be found and used against a student. It can lead to expulsion, loss of a job, rescinded or rejected college admittance or scholarship and, even worse, criminal charges. As you can see, these are serious ramifications you don't want to sweep under the rug. Many platforms have age restrictions (age 13 for most platforms), but these aren't enforced all the time. Ofcom's Children and Parents Media Use and Attitudes report found that 46% of 11-year-olds, 51% of 12-year-olds and 28% of 10-year-olds have a social media profile. Parents must be aware of this so that they can respond and monitor accordingly. Kids at that age are naïve and unaware of the predators waiting to lure them in, and also about how their lack of experience can lead them into a web or trap that costs them opportunities in the future, or even worse, their life.

When it comes to applying for scholarships, which we know can be done as early as kindergarten, scholarship organizations can do a cursory search for inappropriate posts prior to granting an award. This is why we can't wait until a student reaches high school to have this conversation. Posts of the past can resurface and jeopardize those opportunities presented years later.

Let's examine this from a job perspective. According to a survey by Harris Poll for CareerBuilder of hiring managers and human resource professionals, 70% of them admitted that a potential job candidate was not hired because of their social media behavior, such as the posting of inappropriate content and photos. Here are some examples of what may be deemed inappropriate:

- Pictures of a student drinking and partying hard, especially if they are underage
- A video of someone being drunk, carrying out sexual or provocative behavior (wet t-shirts, twerking, thirsty poses, etc.)
- Use of profanity on their page
- Comments that can be deemed as threatening, discriminatory, racist, etc.
- Pictures of them with drugs, drug paraphernalia, or weapons
- Signs of cyberbullying
- Negative comments about their job, boss, school, or a person of authority

Remember that there is no such thing as privacy when it comes to the internet and technology. It's all public, and it always will be. Anything you post or text can be retrieved. They may think what they do on "their" own time is "their" business, but unfortunately that is not the case. Whatever they do "on and off the clock" is still an extension of the brand that their job or school represents.

To make this clear, if their character and behavior contradicts their school's or job's image and brand, they will likely lose any opportunity with them. No company or school wants a person on their roster who will embarrass them and pose a risk to everything they've accomplished. Not only can this behavior preclude them from being hired, but it can also cause them to be fired after the fact. Please educate your child and challenge them to think twice before posting anything on these social media platforms.

Remind them that this is not the place to air their "dirty laundry" and to discuss drama with and about friends, boyfriends, or girlfriends. Schools and scholarship organizations are looking for solid and responsible leaders who consider the costs, can problem solve, and think through all situations. Companies and colleges have the power to make whatever decision they choose as long as it does not violate any federal employment or discriminatory laws. Here are a few examples:

Example 1

One of America's popular bloggers of her time, Heather B. Armstrong was identified as a Forbes 2009 "Most Influential Woman In Media." In 2002, she shared her personal experiences and opinions about the internet company she worked for on her personal blog. As a result, Armstrong lost her web designer and graphic artist job. She was fired. Because of her notoriety, the Free and Urban Dictionary coined the word *dooce*, which means "to be fired from your job because of content on your weblog." Heather is now known as the matriarch of Dooce.com.

Example 2

A University of Richmond football recruit admissions was rescinded due to backlash from a Snapchat video shared from a friend's account in late June 2020. In the video, a racial slur was used by the football player, after which he tells his friend, "Oh wait, you can't put that one up." The video went viral on Twitter, leading to an online petition calling for rescission of his admissions offer. The university issued a statement that the video "did not reflect the university's values or its commitment to a thriving and inclusive community." (The New York Times)

Example 3

A 2020 valedictorian lost her spot at the University of Florida after a Twitter post featuring racist language surfaced. Although the post was over a year old, the derogatory language had been directed at two of her black classmates with a caption that read, "I really try so hard not to be a racist person, but I most definitely am, there's no denying it & it gets the best of me sometimes [sic]." She went on to use expletives and closed out her post with "i want to punch them because they are so [expletive] retarded, anyone within the proximity of them has the possibility of losing brain cells. they're most definitely crack whores & people like them do nothing for society, i swear [sic]." The University of Florida took action, revoked the student's admission and tweeted that the prospective student "who posted racist comments on social media will not be joining the University of Florida community this fall." (The Hill.TV)

Example 4

Dan Leone, a Philadelphia Eagles stadium operations worker, was unhappy with the NFL team's decision to let Brian Dawkins, a safety, go to sign with the Denver Broncos. Leone vented to his pals on Facebook, declaring: "Dan is [expletive] devastated about Dawkins signing with Denver…Dam Eagles R Retarded!!" He later deleted the post, but the Eagles fired him over the phone a few days later. (ESPN)

Example 5

Two young ladies graduated within the top 1% of their high school class and had GPAs above 4.0 and multiple scholarship opportunities. While interviewing for a prestigious university for college admission and full academic scholarships, they were confident in their responses to the interviewing panel.

Unfortunately, the interview took a turn when the last question asked pertained to the girls' Facebook pages and the inappropriate pictures and comments that had been posted previously. As a result, they were immediately disqualified and rejected from being admitted to this top tier university.

There are countless other examples I can share, but I believe that you get the point and the underlying message about privacy on the internet; it simply doesn't exist. Because of these types of scenarios, organizations have created tools, positions, and have teams of people adept at searching for unbecoming posts and messages. It is part of the application process whether you know it or not. According to Proofpoint, in companies with at least 1,000 employees, 10% have disciplined their ranks for violating the rules, while 8% of these organizations have fired at least one employee for egregious violations. Because most people do not read the fine print of their employment agreements and privacy policies to even know that this an occurrence, the best rule of thumb is to not publish anything via the internet you would not want anyone to know about or see.

Our focus here is to share how not to turn the innocuous action of using social media to socially connect into your worst nightmare and let it overshadow the great things accomplished academically and professionally. Social networking has also opened the door to many other risks such as identity theft, the facilitation of pedophilia, harassment, infidelity, and many others. Get informed and put controls in place to protect your child's future. As parents, you have the power to mitigate their risk, level of exposure and vulnerability. You have every right to monitor their accounts, have regular check in discussions, stay in tune with social media trends and technological advancements, and learn about the tools used to hide activity from involved parents. Sites like Internet Safety 101 (www.internetsafety101.org) is a great place to start and a life-changing resource.

SEXTING

The use and application of cell phones has undeniably reached new levels. What used to be a mode of communication for the elite, government, and military officials is now used as a tool for engaging underage youth, tracking their behavior and activities, and facilitating pornography. Cell phones have become a part of our daily lives, like brushing our teeth and putting on clothes. Just as it has enhanced our lives, it has also cost people their lives. We are going to look at one of the risk areas, commonly known as sexting.

In case you are unfamiliar with the term, let's start with the basics. When teens and tweens create provocative and nude, sexual images or videos of themselves using their cell phone's camera, that oftentimes lead to sexting. The action of sharing those images or videos and receiving sexually explicit messages and nude or partially nude images are, by definition, what sexting is.

Internet Safety 101 highlighted a survey completed by the National Campaign to Prevent Teen and Unplanned Pregnancy. This study revealed that when it comes to teens sending or sharing sexually provocative images (nude or seminude) or videos via an electronic device or online, one out of five teens admitted to committing such acts. Because of the nature and implications of these actions, we cannot continue to ignore this topic. It will not only impact their ability to get into college and secure scholarships, but it can also lead to depression, suicide, arrests, possible prosecution, and so on. Please understand that teens and tweens who engage in this illicit activity are essentially facilitating the transmission of child pornography, which is a felony. Because state laws have not caught up to technology, it can lead to serious repercussions such as felony charges. So, again, this is not something to play with.

Everyone needs to be informed, aware, and concerned about the other ramifications of sexting. Kids are sometimes sexting to strangers they meet online, who are often pedophiles; in addition, they are sexting with their boyfriends, girlfriends, and potential companions. Often, they do this as a result of peer pressure from a so-called companion or friend as a means of fitting in or keeping them as a boyfriend or girlfriend. Other times, they do it just for fun. Alternatively, they may have received a sext from a friend concerning a classmate and they decided to also share it with others. Either way, all of these actions are dangerous and illegal.

Parents, get your head out of the sand and discuss this with your kids, on top of monitoring their behavior. If you find such content on your child's phone, do not send it to anybody electronically! That action will now make you part of the trail when an investigation occurs. Immediately take the device and share it with police officials first to protect yourself and your child. It may also be a wise idea to consult an attorney versed in this area to find out what the local laws are in your area beforehand so you can properly prepare. Law officials know that students can be careless and sometimes act recklessly, but the legal system can often tie their hands. Get ahead of this by becoming informed and using sites like Internet Safety 101 to mitigate the risk of occurrence.

This also ties in with the hidden apps discussed in the previous section. The same level of caution applies to videos captured with their phones and shared on platforms like YouTube. Don't allow them to video activity that will land them in a criminal investigation. Nothing is "innocent" about capturing photos or videos involving racy, sexual, or illicit acts or positionings.

To further solidify how real this is, let's close this section out with a few stats from Internet Safety 101 and some of its research partners.

- Out of 68,000 cases of self-generated images studied in 2020, 80% of the cases were of girls between 11 and 13 years of age. (Internet Watch Foundation, April 21, 2021)

- Incidents involving children and sexting increased 183% during the COVID lockdown. This includes girls as young as 6-years old. (SafeToNet, June 24, 2020).

- By the time a child reaches the age of 13, close to 40% of them have either received and/or sent a text that incudes sexual content. (Parenting App Jiminy, December 18, 2019)

Cell phones are well beyond the device used to solely communicate and keep track of your child while at school or participating in extracurricular activities needed to build their college profiles. These tools are essentially an electronic gateway to the world with no boundaries or gatekeepers that keep them out of harm's way. Parents must build upon those controls and actively manage them to protect their child's brand image, life, future, and mental state.

Posing a Child in a State of Nudity or Sexual Conduct

It is illegal for anyone (this includes minors) to knowingly encourage, cause, coerce, solicit, or entice a person under the age of 18 to pose or be shown in a state of nudity or semi-nudity for the sake of photographing them. Clearly, when you see that statistics tell us 12% of girls have felt pressured to send sexually suggestive images and/or messages taken with their cell phone or digital camera, this is a violation of this stature.

Dissemination of Pictures of a Child in a State of Nudity or Sexual Conduct

It is illegal for anyone, including minors, to knowingly send out or disseminate pictures of a person under the age of 18 who is nude, semi-nude, and/or engaged in a sexual act to someone else. Again, when 52% of teens have sent "sexting presents" to their companions and 44% have sent images via a phone in response of one received, they have violated this stature. Going a step further, if a teen girl sends an inappropriate image to her boyfriend and he in return distributes the image to other students and the cycle continues, they will all be in violation and considered someone who willingly disseminated pictures of a minor.

POSSESSION OF CHILD PORNOGRAPHY

When a person knowingly is in possession of a sexually explicit image in any format that displays private parts of the body (genitals, buttocks, or breasts) or simulated sexual acts of a person under the age of 18, this is an illegal act defined as the possession of child pornography. This can include a parent, like in the previous paragraph, who discovered such images on their child's phone and sent it to themselves or another adult. As laws evolve, you want to always exercise an abundance of caution in these situations. Your innocent intent could violate many laws.

Dissemination of Harmful Matter to a Minor

As previously stated, sharing inappropriate images of a minor is illegal. When a person knowingly sends these types of images, the law considers the act to be a "harmful matter" because of its obscene or pornographic nature.

As you can see, this is very serious and many lives are being ruined due to a lack of knowledge and naivety to the fact they can be charged and possibly convicted for criminal behavior that is considered a felony. It is time to wake up and be aware of the risks involved with abusing technology and the intent it was created for. Although there is a growing consensus among lawyers and legislators that the child pornography laws are too blunt for the world of adolescent cyber-culture, the behavior can still cause a student to be expelled from school, fired, and unable to move forward with their career aspirations.

As technology continues to evolve and more and more cases of cyber bullying occur, laws are changing. Parents, please research the laws in your area and educate your child on them to ensure they do not become a victim over what they perceive to be an "innocent" and "harmless" act. Their future depends on this knowledge.

CHAPTER TAKEAWAYS

1. Key Learnings (what you didn't know before):

_____

_____

_____

_____

2. What You Need to Unlearn or Stop Doing:

_____

_____

_____

_____

3. What You Need to Do Next:

_____

_____

_____

_____

CHAPTER 7
BRINGING IT ALL TOGETHER

If you want to be successful....Don't seek success
Seek to become a person of value; Value is in significance

DR. MYLES MUNROE

Your gift will make room for you in the world.

The college and career readiness process and planning for a debt-free education is no small task, nor is it an easy one. It is a huge undertaking with layers and layers of coordination, time management, organization, studying, hard work, and discipline. Then repeat. The process is tedious and nerve racking at times, especially since the pandemic. Rules of engagement are changing and the game is shifting quickly. If you know how to navigate the varying landmines and master the game, the result supersedes the stress and energy executed.

The level of success is indicative of one's knowledge base, the time they start, and the resources they choose to invest in. Doing this alone without knowledge of how the game is played will exaggerate the stress level a family will incur. It is my hope that the information in this book will, at minimum, give parents the foundational knowledge needed to give them a fighting chance at winning the game. Along with the knowledge base, families need to understand the strategy aspect and that is what we give our clients. Now, that doesn't mean you can't win some battles by applying the information in this book. I implore you to take action today. You and your child's financial future and life depends on it.

Getting started, starting sooner, and applying the tools in this book can be the difference between $10,000 and $30,000 per year, if not more. When I think about the GoFundMe accounts posted by families needing $10,000 and $20,000 in two months so that their baby can go to college, having the level of insight in this book could have eliminated the need to resort to such measures. If you are still wondering if it's worth it, just imagine what your life and stress level would be if your child was in college with their studies fully funded. It would mean that you don't have to worry about them coming back home and living off of you because they ran out of money and can't afford to live on their own. It would also mean that they have a greater chance of accomplishing their career goals and making a positive difference in the world. Another benefit to consider is your ability (and their ability) to buy what you want when you want it because you're not strapped for cash due to high student loan debt that has a balance that never decreases.

The choice is yours.

I've seen it happen for my clients with COA as high as $75,000. This, too, can happen to you when you learn how to play the game and position your child as a money and opportunity magnet. You just have to be willing to put in the work and consistently commit to the process. Congratulations on investing in your child's future by purchasing this book. Please take action today and start applying the knowledge shared within it.

It is my hope that you find the information in this book valuable and a practical tool for use along your family's journey to post-secondary success. Be sure to look at the Appendix while checking out the workbook and college planning journal we offer. They all work together to drive action and results. If you find that you need personalized help, visit thecollegeprepboss.com for information on our VIP Coaching Programs that have helped attract families over well over $40 million dollars in scholarships.

We'd love to hear from you, so share your story and connect with us on all social media platforms.

CHAPTER TAKEAWAYS

1. Key Learnings (what you didn't know before):

_____

_____

_____

_____

2. What You Need to Unlearn or Stop Doing:

_____

_____

_____

_____

3. What You Need to Do Next:

_____

_____

_____

_____

APPENDIX

PREPARING FOR THE PSAT, SAT, AND ACT COLLEGE EXAMINATION PREP TIMELINE

8TH GRADE/FRESHMAN

- Build Vocabulary & Reading Comprehension: vocabulary exercises, word games, etc.
- Study ACT/SAT & testing strategies
- Take Pre/AP (Advanced Placement) & IB (International Baccalaureate) Courses

SOPHOMORE

- Summer before:
  - Continue to build vocabulary & reading comprehension skills
  - Study ACT/SAT & testing strategies
  - Enroll in ACT/SAT test prep class
- Fall:
  - Take Aspire (Preliminary ACT) and PSAT
  - Take ACT/SAT
  - Take AP & IB Courses
- Spring:
  - Take ACT/SAT
  - Take AP & IB Courses
  - Take AP/IB Tests

JUNIOR

- Summer before:

  ○ ACT/SAT Test Preparation Class/Refresh

- Fall:

  ○ Take PSAT: qualifying test for National Merit Scholarship

  ○ Take AP & IB Courses

  ○ Take ACT/SAT

- Spring:

  ○ Take AP/IB subject area tests

  ○ Take ACT/SAT (goal: last time)

SENIOR

- Fall:

  ○ Take SAT/ACT (only if needed to raise score a few points)

  ○ Send scores to colleges

- Spring:

  ○ Register and take AP/IB subject area tests

9-YEAR COLLEGE & CAREER READINESS TIMELINE

MIDDLE SCHOOL

Status S-Started I-In Progress C-Complete NA	Item	Task Item	Timing
		9 Year College Preparation Timeline	
	I.	**4th - 6th Grade Year**	
	a	Start researching college and career enrichment programs for after school and summer months to enroll in	June - September
	b	Start or continue researching scholarships/private sources to create a scholarship tracking spreadsheet - Apply when Applicable	Immediately
	c	Meet with school counselors regularly to review courses - Seek out honors and advanced classes early	August - September & March-May
	d	Learn about colleges - Visit schools and discuss admissions and financial aid process for exposure	May-June
	e	Sit Down as a family to discuss college planning and financial aid	June-July
	f	Construct a year around reading plan to develop vocabulary and writing skills	January
	g	Start saving for college - if not already	Immediately
	II.	**7th & 8th Grade Year**	
	a	Start researching and investigating possible careers and schools	August - September
	b	Consult middle and high school counselors on college ready courses for enrollment	August - September
	c	Learn about financial aid offering available at school from school Counselor	May-June
	d	Get involved in extracurricular activities	
	e	Sit Down as a Family to Discuss College Plan and Financial Aid. If this is the first time, create a plan.	June-July
	f	Start saving for college - if not already	Immediately
	g	Continue researching scholarships/private sources to create a scholarship tracking spreadsheet - Apply when Applicable	Immediately
	h	Construct a year around reading plan to develop vocabulary and writing skills	January
	i	Prepare for ACT/SAT/PSAT Tests - Resources ACT/SAT Books, Websites, Classes, etc	Year Around

HIGH SCHOOL: 9TH AND 10TH GRADE

Status S-Started I-In Progress C-Complete NA	Item	Task Item	Timing
	III.	**9th Grade Year**	
	a	Get Involved in Extracurricular Activities	Immediately
	b	Build a flexible schedule that includes studying, extracurricular activities and other interests	August - June
	c	Develop a 4-Year Schedule of Classes per college eligibility requirements for the most competitive college on the list - Include AP/IB Courses	July-August
	d	Continue working to keep grades up	August - June
	e	Take an Interest/Career Assessment to discover possible career matches	July-August
	f	Start Developing a resume and/or portfolio of accomplishments, awards and activities	October - November
	g	Review college plan and financial aid with family, tribe and school counselor	May-June
	h	Look for volunteer opportunities	August - June
	i	Apply for summer job, internship and/or Program related to selected career field, where possible.	March-May
	j	Prepare for ACT/SAT/PSAT Tests - Resources ACT/SAT Books, Websites, Classes, etc	May-August
	k	Create a ACT/SAT/PSAT Study Plan	May-August
	l	Continue researching scholarships/private sources to create a scholarship tracking spreadsheet - Apply when Applicable	Year Around
	IV.	**10th Grade Year**	
	a	Re-evaluate course selection to ensure alignment w/college eligibility and career Focus	August-September
	b	Continue working to keep grades up	August-June
	c	If pursuing athletics, check NCAA Requirements and cultivate relationships with college coaches/athletic directors - create athletic performance reels	August-May
	d	Review CommonApp website for new application/Eessay prompts - practice writing essays	August
	e	Register for ACT/SAT test you plan to sit for that school year	August
	f	Prepare for PSAT	September-October
	g	Take the PSAT	October
	h	Continue college savings	Year around
	i	Stay Active in volunteer activities	Year around
	j	Stay active in extracurricular activities	Year around
	k	Apply for summer job, internship and/or program related roles to selected career field	March-May
	l	Continue preparing for ACT/SAT/PSAT tests - execute resources and study plan	Year around
	m	Continue searchinfg for scholarships and Update the scholarship tracker - Apply when applicable	Year around
	n	Enroll in AP/IB Courses	Feb-April
	o	Take AP/IB Tests	May

HIGH SCHOOL: 11TH GRADE

Status S-Started I-In Progress C-Complete NA	Item	Task Item	Timing
	V.	**11th Grade Year**	
	a	Re-evaluate course selection to ensure alignment w/college requirements and career focus	August-September
	b	Continue college savings	Year around
	n	If you plan to play sports in college, reach out and track communications with coaches	June-September
	o	Apply for NCAA eligibility via the clearinghouse and submit video highlight reels	August
	c	Start making college visits - if you haven't already	September-October
	d	Attend college informational sessions	September-December
	e	Compile a list of schools of interest, pertinent data and request an admissions packet, if applicable	October-November
	f	Talk with Admission Representative to Determine Available Institutional Scholarships	October-November
	g	Continue Preparing for ACT/SAT/PSAT Tests - Execute Resources and Study Plan	Year around
	h	Continue Scholarship Search and Update the Scholarship Tracking Book - Apply when Applicable	Year around
	i	Sign-up to Take the SAT/ACT	August-December
	k	Consider Taking College Prep Courses in the Summer	May-August
	l	Start Asking Teachers for College Recommendations	January
	s	Apply for Summer Job, Internship and/or Program related to Selected Career Field	January-March
	q	Stay Active in Volunteer Activities	Year around
	r	Stay Active in Extracurricular Activities	Year around
	m	Narrow your college application list down and plan visits	March-April
	n	Close out school year meeting with counselor to review accomplishments, summer plans and final preparation for senior year	April - May
	o	Take AP/IB Tests	May
	p	Start Working on College Essays	May-August
	q	Visit Colleges	April-June
	r	Discuss Final School Selection with Parents and Discuss Financial Plan	May-August

HIGH SCHOOL: 12TH GRADE

Status S-Started I-In Progress C-Complete NA	Item	Task Item	Timing
	V.	**12th Grade Year**	
	a	Create a filing and tracking system and binder for in preparation for the financial aid and college admissions process	June - July
	b	Visit colleges	June - July
	c	Finalize list of schools you will seek Admissions from	June - July
	d	Determine which admissions approach you will pursue: early decision, early action, rolling, or regular	June - July
	e	Register to re-take the SAT or ACT (if necessary) during the first offerings (August)	June - July
	f	Identify and notify teachers, coaches, and employers you plan to seek letters of recommendations from - Provide student resume with application deadlines	July-August
	g	Review college applications, assemble a checklist of requirements and finalize all required essays	July-August
	h	Parents and Seniors, set up formal meeting with counselor to review college admissions timeline, recommendation, and transcript request process to mitigate delays	July-August
	i	Make Final Touches to Portfolio, Resume and/or Brag Book	August-September
	j	Create a Weekly Action Plan that will Guide you on Tasks Needing Completion for Admission, Scholarship, Financial Aid Application	September-October
	k	Start Filling Out College Applications - Track Deadlines	August
	l	Continue Scholarship Application Process	Year around
	m	Continue Working Hard and Maintain Good Grades	Year around
	n	If pursuing athletic scholarships, continue managing the relationships and update targeted coaches of application plan and accomplishments	September-October
	o	Register for a Federal Student Aid Personal ID (parent and student)	September-October
	p	Apply for FAFSA	October
	q	Check and verify that your transcripts were submitted and received by all colleges applied to	October-December
	r	Check and verify that your ACT/SAT scores were submitted and received by all colleges applied to	October-December
	s	Complete separate scholarship applications at school beyond the FAFSA	October-December
	t	Stay On Top of All Due Dates	Year around
	u	Contact the financial aid office of to get an understanding of how they will treat outside scholarships you win	November-December
	v	Submit Your Mid-Year High School Transcript to Any College that Require this Information	November-December
	w	Track acceptance letters	November-March
	x	Track, review and compare financial aid award offerings	December-April
	y	Apply for summer job, internship and/or summer enrichment program related to career field	February-May
	z	Prepare and take AP/IB Exams	February-April
	aa	Make an Enrollment Decision and Send Appropriate Deposits	April-May
	bb	Take AP/IB Tests	May
	cc	Sign up for summer orientation for incoming freshmen	May
	dd	Send Final Transcripts to Your Selected College	May
	ee	Send Thank You Letters to your College Support Team (Counselors, Teachers, Coaches, etc)	Year around

ABOUT THE AUTHOR

Tameka L. Williamson is a passionate and dedicated motivational speaker, coach, and executive leadership strategist. She is the multi-award-winning and bestselling author of *Parents, Send Your Child to College for Free*; *Getting A Full Ride*; and *A Road to Success: The College Planning and Preparatory Guide*, as well as a contributor to two influential faith-based and educational collaborations. Her gifts run the veritable gamut when it comes to teaching academic hopefuls and their parents how to "Kill The College Game" with her insightful, groundbreaking, and revolutionary approach.

Tameka has been featured in *Forbes*, *Huffington Post*, *The Examiner*, and *Lifetime Moms*, among many other respected publications. Her life's passion is focused on improving the lives of students and leaders by connecting them to pathways of upward mobility so they can live their best lives personally and professionally. She lives in Atlanta, Georgia.

Learn more at www.tamekawilliamson.com